ATLAS OF THE EUROPEAN REFORMATIONS

Atlas of the European Reformations

by Tim Dowley

Cartographer Nick Rowland FRGS

Fortress Press
Minneapolis

Cover design: Alisha Lofgren
Cover image (*clockwise from the top*):
© Jose Antonio Sánchez Reyes / Dreamstime.com; © Hai
Huy Ton That / Dreamstime.com; © Bkaiser / Dreamstime.
com; © Tonino Corso / Dreamstime.com; © Hans Klamm /
Dreamstime.com; © Neil Harrison / Dreamstime.com;
© Stbernardstudio / Dreamstime.com

Library of Congress Cataloging-in-Publication Data
Print ISBN: 978-1-4514-9969-8
eBook ISBN: 978-1-5064-0291-8

The paper used in this publication meets the minimum
requirements of American National Standard for Information
Sciences — Permanence of Paper for Printed Library Materials,
ANSI Z329.48-1984.

Manufactured in China

A map does not just chart, it unlocks and formulates meaning; it forms bridges between here and there, between disparate ideas that we did not know were previously connected.

REIF LARSEN

History is a clock that people use to tell their political and cultural time of day. It is a compass they use to find themselves on the map of human geography. It tells them where they are...

JOHN HENRIK CLARKE

Contents

Part 3: Catholic Reform and Counter-Reformation

Part 4: Early Modern Europe

List of maps

This atlas has been designed to examine the origins, background, beginning and spread of the Protestant Reformation. It looks at the repercussions of that movement on Europe and the wider world. The Catholic Reformation and Counter-Reformation are covered in similar depth and breadth, as are the political and military conflicts arising in part from these theological and ecclesiastical changes. An exhaustive timeline has also been included to provide a useful chronology of events.

We believe this atlas breaks new ground in being a digitally-designed and comprehensive historical atlas of the religious history of the early modern period in Europe and the wider world.

All research and writing has been undertaken by Tim Dowley. The cartography is the work of Cambridge-based Nick Rowland. Page layout and design has been carried out by Trevor Bounford of Bounford.com, while the index and gazetteer have been compiled by Christopher Pipe of Watermark. The academic consultant is Dr Richard Snoddy, London School of Theology.

March 2015

Timeline AD 1300–1700

1302 Pope Boniface VIII (r. 1294–1303) issues papal bull *Unam sanctam*

1304–74 Francesco Petrarch, Italian scholar and poet

c.1308–21 Dante Alighieri writes *The Divine Comedy*

1309–77 Papacy moves to Avignon, beginning 'Babylonian Captivity'

c. 1330–84 John Wyclif, English reformer

1337–1453 Hundred Years' War between England and France

1346–53 Black Death in Europe

c. 1369–1415 Jan Hus, Czech reformer

1378–1418 Great Papal Schism: between 2, then 3, simultaneous popes

c. 1380–1471 Thomas à Kempis, author of *The Imitation of Christ*

1382–95 Wyclif's Bible: Middle English vernacular translations

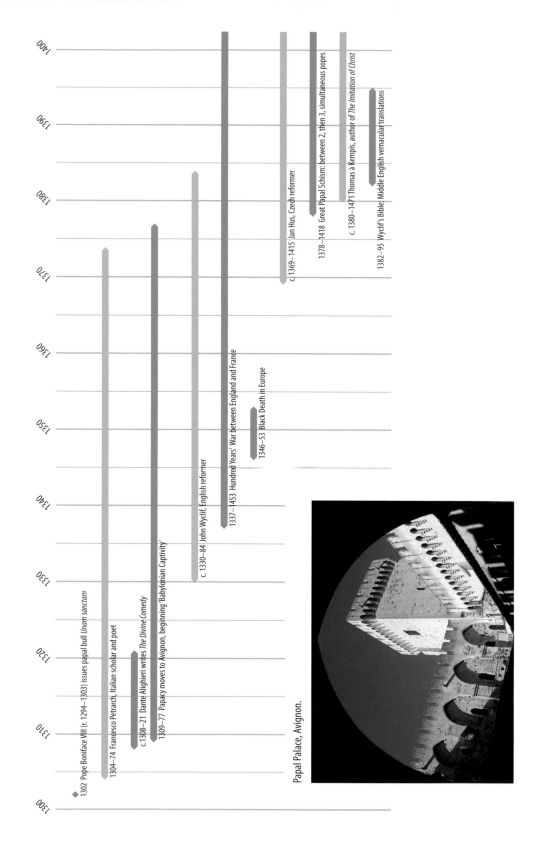

Papal Palace, Avignon.

1337–1453 Hundred 'Years' War between England and France

c. 1369–1415 Jan Hus, Czech reformer

1378–1418 Great Papal Schism: between 2, then 3, simultaneous popes

c. 1380–1471 Thomas à Kempis, author of *The Imitation of Christ*

1414–18 Council of Constance ends papal schism, condemns Hus

1452–1519 Leonardo da Vinci, Italian painter and inventor

1453 Constantinople falls to the Ottoman Empire

1454/5 Gutenberg Bible published

1466–1536 Erasmus of Rotterdam, Christian humanist

1471–1528 Albrecht Dürer, German artist

1478 Spanish Inquisition established

1482–1531 Johannes Oecolampadius, German reformer

1483–1546 Martin Luther, German reformer

1484–1531 Huldrych Zwingli, Swiss reformer

1489–1556 Thomas Cranmer, Archbishop of Canterbury and reformer

1491–1556 Ignatius Loyola, founder of the Jesuits

1491–1551 Martin Bucer, Protestant reformer in Strasbourg

1492 Spain reconquers Granada

1492 Columbus lands in Bahamas

r. 1492–1503 Pope Alexander VI

1493 Pope divides New World between Spain and Portugal

c. 1495 da Vinci's *The Last Supper*

1496–1561 Menno Simons, Anabaptist leader

c. 1497–1543 Hans Holbein, German painter

1497 John Cabot discovers Newfoundland

1497–9 Vasco de Gama finds sea route to India

1498 Savonarola burned for heresy, Florence

c. 1498–1526 Conrad Grebel, Swiss radical reformer

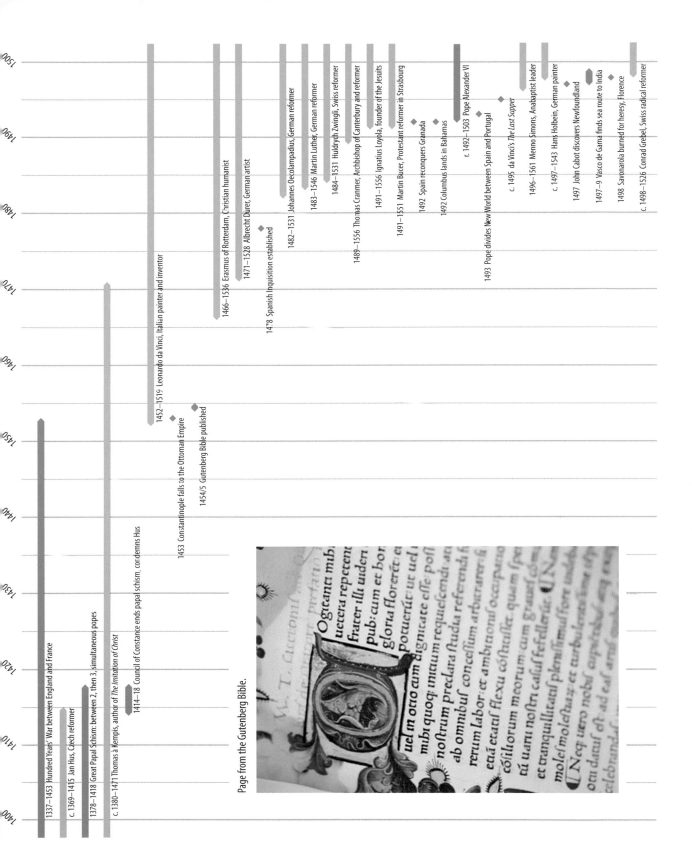

Page from the Gutenberg Bible.

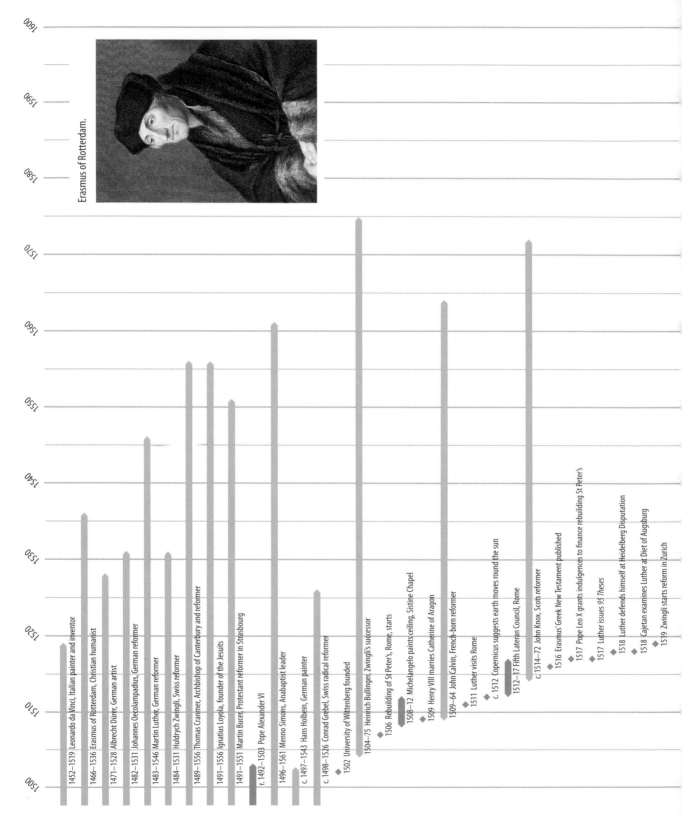

Erasmus of Rotterdam.

1452–1519 Leonardo da Vinci, Italian painter and inventor

1466–1536 Erasmus of Rotterdam, Christian humanist

1471–1528 Albrecht Dürer, German artist

1482–1531 Johannes Oecolampadius, German reformer

1483–1546 Martin Luther, German reformer

1484–1531 Huldrych Zwingli, Swiss reformer

1489–1556 Thomas Cranmer, Archbishop of Canterbury and reformer

1491–1556 Ignatius Loyola, founder of the Jesuits

1491–1551 Martin Bucer, Protestant reformer in Strasbourg

r. 1492–1503 Pope Alexander VI

1496–1561 Menno Simons, Anabaptist leader

c. 1497–1543 Hans Holbein, German painter

c. 1498–1526 Conrad Grebel, Swiss radical reformer

1502 University of Wittenberg founded

1504–75 Heinrich Bullinger, Zwingli's successor

1506 Rebuilding of St Peter's, Rome, starts

1508–12 Michelangelo paints ceiling, Sistine Chapel

1509 Henry VIII marries Catherine of Aragon

1509–64 John Calvin, French-born reformer

1511 Luther visits Rome

c. 1512 Copernicus suggests earth moves round the sun

1512–17 Fifth Lateran Council, Rome

c. 1514–72 John Knox, Scots reformer

1516 Erasmus' Greek New Testament published

1517 Pope Leo X grants indulgences to finance rebuilding St Peter's

1517 Luther issues 95 Theses

1518 Luther defends himself at Heidelberg Disputation

1518 Cajetan examines Luther at Diet of Augsburg

1519 Zwingli starts reform in Zurich

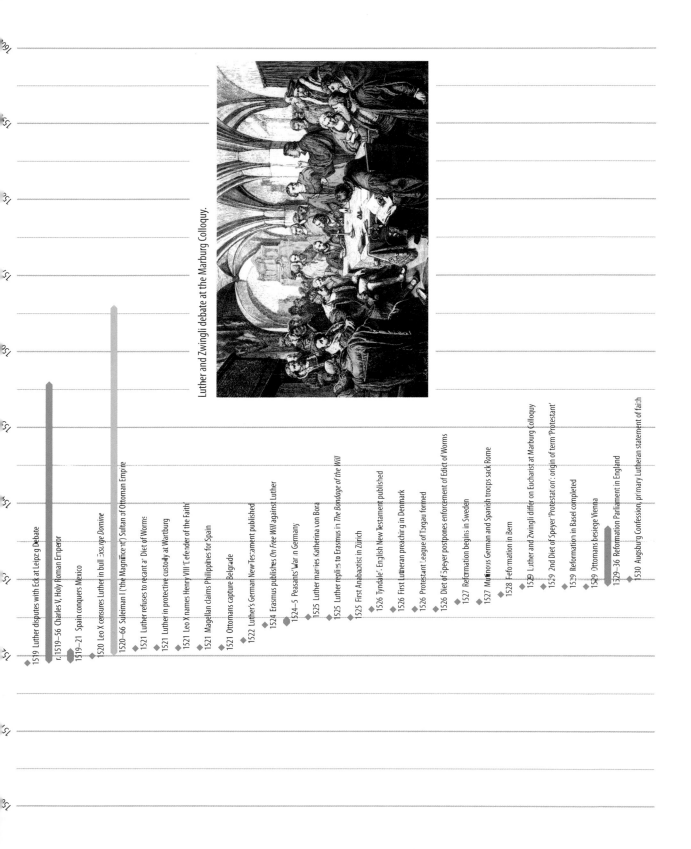

Luther and Zwingli debate at the Marburg Colloquy.

1519 Luther disputes with Eck at Leipzig Debate

r. 1519–56 Charles V, Holy Roman Emperor

1519–21 Spain conquers Mexico

1520 Leo X censures Luther in bull *Exsurge Domine*

1520–66 Suleiman I ('the Magnificent') Sultan of Ottoman Empire

1521 Luther refuses to recant at Diet of Worms

1521 Luther in protective custody at Wartburg

1521 Leo X names Henry VIII 'Defender of the Faith'

1521 Magellan claims Philippines for Spain

1521 Ottomans capture Belgrade

1522 Luther's German New Testament published

1524 Erasmus publishes *On Free Will* against Luther

1524–5 Peasants' War in Germany

1525 Luther marries Katharina von Bora

1525 Luther replies to Erasmus in *The Bondage of the Will*

1525 First Anabaptist in Zürich

1526 Tyndale's English New Testament published

1526 First Lutheran preaching in Denmark

1526 Protestant League of Torgau formed

1526 Diet of Speyer postpones enforcement of Edict of Worms

1527 Reformation begins in Sweden

1527 Mutinous German and Spanish troops sack Rome

1528 Reformation in Bern

1529 Luther and Zwingli differ on Eucharist at Marburg Colloquy

1529 2nd Diet of Speyer 'Protestation': origin of term 'Protestant'

1529 Reformation in Basel completed

1529 Ottomans besiege Vienna

1529–36 Reformation Parliament in England

1530 Augsburg Confession, primary Lutheran statement of faith

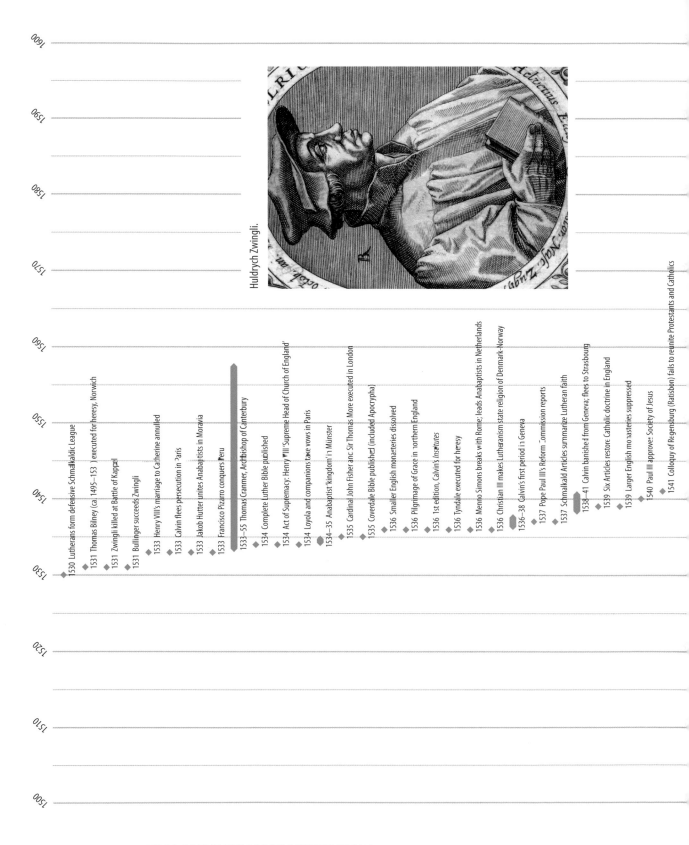

Huldrych Zwingli.

1530 Lutherans form defensive Schmalkaldic League

1531 Thomas Bilney (ca. 1495–153) executed for heresy, Norwich

1531 Zwingli killed at Battle of Kappel

1531 Bullinger succeeds Zwingli

1533 Henry VIII's marriage to Catherine annulled

1533 Calvin flees persecution in Paris

1533 Jakob Hutter unites Anabaptists in Moravia

1533 Francisco Pizarro conquers Peru

1533–55 Thomas Cranmer, Archbishop of Canterbury

1534 Complete Luther Bible published

1534 Act of Supremacy: Henry VIII 'Supreme Head of Church of England'

1534 Loyola and companions take vows in Paris

1534–35 Anabaptist 'kingdom' in Münster

1535 Cardinal John Fisher and Sir Thomas More executed in London

1535 Coverdale Bible published (included Apocrypha)

1536 Smaller English monasteries dissolved

1536 Pilgrimage of Grace in northern England

1536 1st edition, Calvin's *Institutes*

1536 Tyndale executed for heresy

1536 Menno Simons breaks with Rome; leads Anabaptists in Netherlands

1536 Christian III makes Lutheranism state religion of Denmark-Norway

1536–38 Calvin's first period in Geneva

1537 Pope Paul III's Reform Commission reports

1537 Schmalkald Articles summarize Lutheran faith

1538–41 Calvin banished from Geneva; flees to Strasbourg

1539 Six Articles restore Catholic doctrine in England

1539 Larger English monasteries suppressed

1540 Paul III approves Society of Jesus

1541 Colloquy of Regensburg (Ratisbon) fails to reunite Protestants and Catholics

1542 Francis Xavier (1506–52) arrives in Goa

1542 Paul III establishes permanent Inquisition

1543 Luther writes *On the Jews and Their Lies*

1545–47 First session of Council of Trent

1546 George Wishart, Scots reformer, burnt at stake

1547–53 Edward VI reigns in England

1548 Augsburg Interim

1549 Consensus Tigurinus document by Calvin and Bullinger

1549 First English Prayer Book published

1549 Xavier arrives in Japan

1551–52 2nd session of Council of Trent

1552 Bartolomé de Las Casas publishes *A Short Account of the Destruction of the Indies*

1553 Anti-trinitarian Michael Servetus executed, Geneva

1553–58 Mary Tudor reigns in England – Edwardian Reformation reversed

1555 Peace of Augsburg ends first religious war

1555 Augsburg Settlement allows rulers to decide religion of their region

1555 Johann Sleidan publishes first history of Reformation

1556 Thomas Cranmer executed

1558–1603 Elizabeth I reigns in England

1558 Act of Supremacy: Elizabeth 'Supreme Governor of Church in England'

1558 Final edition of Calvin's *Institutes*

1558 John Knox returns to Scotland

1560 Geneva Bible published; first printed with verse divisions

1561 Colloquy of Poissy

1561 Belgic Confession of Reformed faith

1552–63 3rd Session of Council of Trent

1562 Teresa (1515–1582) founds reformed convent at Avila

1562–98 Wars of Religion in France

1563 Heidelberg Catechism of Reformed churches

Council of Trent.

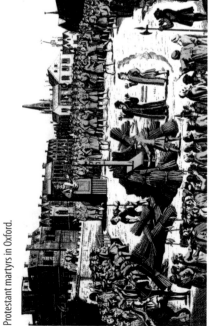

Protestant martyrs in Oxford.

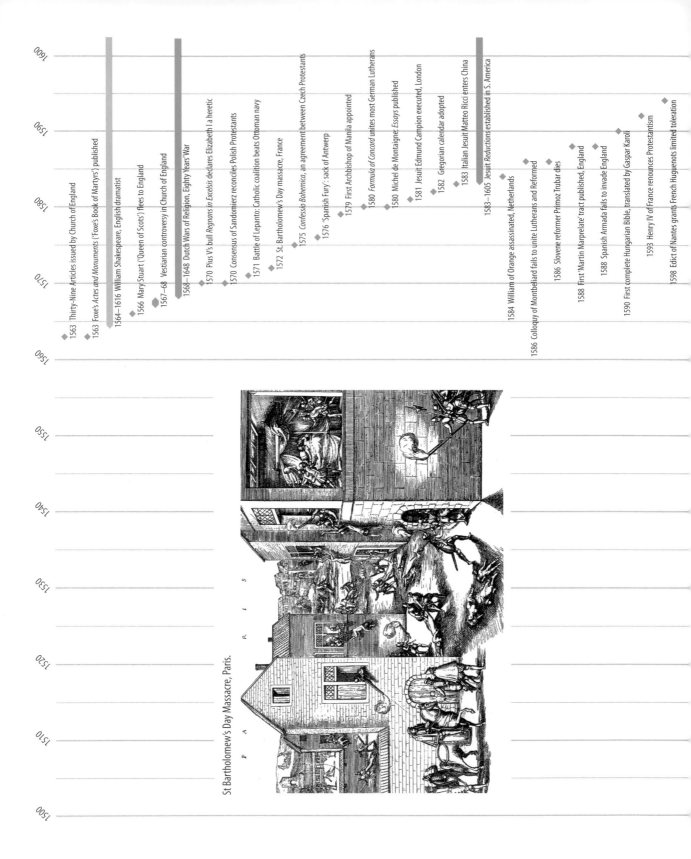

Timeline markers:

1563 Thirty-Nine Articles issued by Church of England

1563 Foxe's *Acts and Monuments* ('Foxe's Book of Martyrs') published

1564–1616 William Shakespeare, English dramatist

1566 Mary Stuart ('Queen of Scots') flees to England

1567–68 Vestiarian controversy in Church of England

1568–1648 Dutch Wars of Religion, Eighty Years' War

1570 Pius V's bull *Regnans in Excelsis* declares Elizabeth I a heretic

1570 Consensus of Sandomierz reconciles Polish Protestants

1571 Battle of Lepanto: Catholic coalition beats Ottoman navy

1572 St. Bartholomew's Day massacre, France

1575 *Confessio Bohemica*, an agreement between Czech Protestants

1576 'Spanish Fury': sack of Antwerp

1579 First Archbishop of Manila appointed

1580 *Formula of Concord* unites most German Lutherans

1580 Michel de Montaigne: *Essays* published

1581 Jesuit Edmund Campion executed, London

1582 Gregorian calendar adopted

1583 Italian Jesuit Matteo Ricci enters China

1583–1605 Jesuit *Reductions* established in S. America

1584 William of Orange assassinated, Netherlands

1586 Colloquy of Montbéliard fails to unite Lutherans and Reformed

1586 Slovene reformer Primož Trubar dies

1588 First 'Martin Marprelate' tract published, England

1588 Spanish Armada fails to invade England

1590 First complete Hungarian Bible, translated by Gaspar Károli

1593 Henry IV of France renounces Protestantism

1598 Edict of Nantes grants French Huguenots limited toleration

St Bartholomew's Day Massacre, Paris.

18   ATLAS OF THE EUROPEAN REFORMATIONS

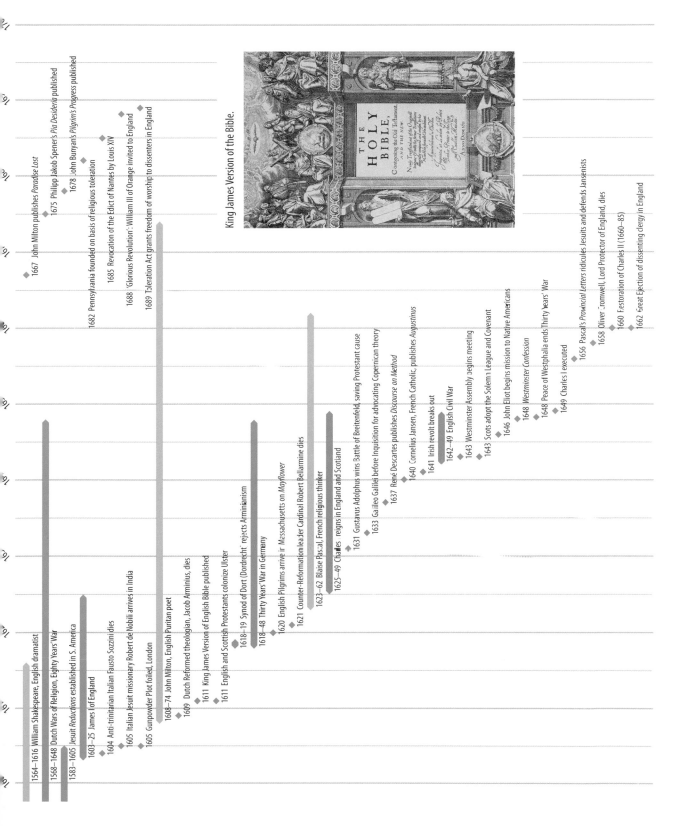

King James Version of the Bible.

1564–1616 William Shakespeare, English dramatist

1568–1648 Dutch Wars of Religion, Eighty Years' War

1583–1605 Jesuit *Reductions* established in S. America

1603–25 James I of England

1604 Anti-trinitarian Italian Fausto Sozzini dies

1605 Italian Jesuit missionary Robert de Nobili arrives in India

1605 Gunpowder Plot foiled, London

1608–74 John Milton, English Puritan poet

1609 Dutch Reformed theologian, Jacob Arminius, dies

1611 King James Version of English Bible published

1611 English and Scottish Protestants colonize Ulster

1618–19 Synod of Dort (Dordrecht) rejects Arminianism

1618–48 Thirty Years' War in Germany

1620 English Pilgrims arrive in Massachusetts on *Mayflower*

1621 Counter-Reformation leader Cardinal Robert Bellarmine dies

1623–62 Blaise Pascal, French religious thinker

1625–49 Charles I reigns in England and Scotland

1631 Gustavus Adolphus wins Battle of Breitenfeld, saving Protestant cause

1633 Galileo Galilei before Inquisition for advocating Copernican theory

1637 René Descartes publishes *Discourse on Method*

1640 Cornelius Jansen, French Catholic, publishes *Augustinus*

1641 Irish revolt breaks out

1642–49 English Civil War

1643 Westminster Assembly begins meeting

1643 Scots adopt the Solemn League and Covenant

1646 John Eliot begins mission to Native Americans

1648 *Westminster Confession*

1648 Peace of Westphalia ends Thirty Years' War

1649 Charles I executed

1656 Pascal's *Provincial Letters* ridicules Jesuits and defends Jansenists

1658 Oliver Cromwell, Lord Protector of England, dies

1660 Restoration of Charles II (1660–85)

1662 Great Ejection of dissenting clergy in England

1667 John Milton publishes *Paradise Lost*

1675 Philipp Jakob Spener's *Pia Desideria* published

1678 John Bunyan's *Pilgrim's Progress* published

1682 Pennsylvania founded on basis of religious toleration

1685 Revocation of the Edict of Nantes by Louis XIV

1688 'Glorious Revolution': William III of Orange invited to England

1689 Toleration Act grants freedom of worship to dissenters in England

Introduction

Between 1350 and 1650 the church in Western Europe experienced significant administrative, moral, and doctrinal reform that brought major changes to the church. These reforms were accompanied by conflict between those committed to the beliefs and practices of the medieval church and those persuaded that major doctrinal and moral reform was necessary. Conflict also arose between those committed to different approaches to reform and to different theologies.

This Reformation resulted in a lasting schism in the church in Western Europe that had essentially remained unified for more than one thousand years. The existence of more than one Christian church was difficult to accept after a millennium of religious unity, and only reluctantly was it acknowledged when it became increasingly clear that neither dialogue nor suppression could restore the church's unity. Religious divisions – together with political, social, and economic factors – led to military conflict that plagued Europe between 1550 and 1648.

The first section of this atlas surveys the pre-Reformation period: the setting in which the events took place, late medieval society, the role of the church in that society, and the various reform movements of the late Middle Ages. Although the late medieval church met the religious needs of society more adequately than many historians have been willing to concede, people were sufficiently alienated from the church to support the Protestant Reformation.

The second section of this book examines the outbreak of the sixteenth-century Reformation. Martin Luther was of course the primary protagonist in the events that resulted in this lasting schism in the church, believing that the teachings of the church had been distorted during the Middle Ages and needed to be brought back into line with Scripture. There soon appeared a number of different reform movements and a great expansion of the Reformation churches. Lutheranism spread through much of Germany and Scandinavia, and new urban movements appeared in Switzerland and Germany. Radical reform movements sprang up throughout Europe, led by people who rejected the 'Magisterial Reformers' who worked with the magistrates or rulers. In Geneva, John Calvin led a reform movement that was soon imitated in much of Europe. Henry VIII initiated a Reformation in England for reasons that had little to do with church reform, but the English church also experienced a Protestant Reformation which reached fruition in the reign of Henry's daughter, Elizabeth. A Protestant Reformation was also firmly established in Scotland.

The Roman Catholic Church was stimulated to reform itself – and also to respond to the rapid growth of Protestantism – movements which are covered in section three. When attempts to heal the breach between the Church of Rome and the growing Protestant movement failed, the papacy called the reforming Council of Trent, which defined the theology of the medieval church in opposition to Protestantism and encouraged moral and spiritual reform within the Roman Catholic Church. The discovery of the Americas led to a new interest in spreading the gospel abroad. The Society of Jesus – the Jesuits, founded by Ignatius Loyola – took the lead within the Catholic Church and sent missionaries to the Americas, India, China, and Japan. Protestants attempted to bring the gospel to Native Americans in the English colonies.

One result of the competing reform movements was theological and military conflict, dealt with in the final section of this atlas. In addition to theological conflicts between Protestants and Catholics, Lutherans, Zwinglians, and Calvinists engaged in ferocious debates, and there were also deep divisions within both Lutheranism and Calvinism, while all parties were critical of the Anabaptists and persecuted them. For their part, Anabaptists were divided among themselves and on occasion resorted to violence in pursuing their objectives.

During the second century of the Reformation era, Germany, France, the Netherlands, and England were all convulsed by religious wars. When neither side was able to overcome the other, they had eventually to agree to compromise settlements, dividing the respective areas between the competing confessions. Only the English Civil War, fought between Protestants, had a different result. The Peace of Westphalia of 1648, which ended the Thirty Years' War, is a clear concluding point for the Reformation era on the European continent; in England it comes ten years later, as the Civil War was followed by the restoration of the Stuart dynasty in 1660.

Part 1

Before the
Reformation

*O quam cito transit
gloria mundi.*

Oh how quickly the
world's glory passes away!

THOMAS À KEMPIS

The Rise of Learning

During the age of Charlemagne and the tenth and eleventh centuries, education in Christian Europe was based mainly in monasteries and cathedral schools – largely the former until the eleventh century. A learned monk would teach novices (new monks) and if he were well known adult monks from other houses would also come to study under him. Other young men from wealthy families would be sent to study under a monastic tutor.

By the twelfth century, cathedral schools had overtaken the monastic establishments. The chancellor – chief cathedral dignitary after the bishop and dean – taught the seven liberal arts and theology to advanced students, while other teachers instructed younger scholars in Latin grammar. Most students were destined to become clerics. A licence to teach, given by the chancellor, was the predecessor of a university degree. During the eleventh century, the leading cathedral schools in northern Europe were at Laon, Paris, Chartres, and Cologne. Debates there reawakened intellectual life in Europe, drawing on the philosophy of ancient Greece, the Bible, and the teachings of the early Christian writers.

First universities

The cathedral schools culminated in the founding of the first universities. The term *universitas* was used to describe a guild or corporation of teachers or scholars who banded together. A city with a well-known cathedral might become the centre for a number of schools. At first scholars rented rooms and students would pay to come and listen to their lectures. Guilds of professors organized the universities of northern Europe, while in Italy the students themselves formed the guilds. The first universities obtained a charter from the pope; those established later applied to the secular ruler.

The gradual development of universities makes it difficult to date them precisely, but among the first were Bologna, Paris, Salerno, Oxford, Cambridge, Montpellier, Padua, Salamanca, and Toulouse. The universities taught the seven liberal arts – a late Roman curriculum that included grammar, logic, rhetoric, arithmetic, geometry, astronomy, and music. However logic, or philosophy, tended to dominate undergraduate education. Graduate faculties taught medicine, law, and theology.

Medieval universities were relatively small by modern standards, the largest having between 3,000 and 4,000 students. At Paris, a boy could begin his studies at the age of twelve, but the privilege of lecturing on theology was not granted until a man (there were, of course, no female students) was thirty-five.

Paris was the most important place of learning, adopted by both Franciscans and Dominicans as their main training centre. Major scholars of this period who studied or taught at Paris include William of Ockham (c. 1288–c. 1348), Anselm of Bec (1033–1109), Peter Abelard (1079–1142), Peter Lombard (1100–60), Albertus Magnus (c. 1200–80), Duns Scotus (c. 1265–1308), Thomas Aquinas (1225–74), and Lothar of Segni (later Pope Innocent III, r. 1198–1216). Their legacy, a systematic account known as 'scholasticism', attempted to harmonize the theology of Augustine with the philosophy of classical Greek thinkers, especially Aristotle. The synthesis of Catholic dogma and reasoning by logic was the achievement of Aquinas in his *Summa Theologiae*, a cornerstone of future Catholic theology – though some of his own teachings were listed in the Condemnations of 1277.

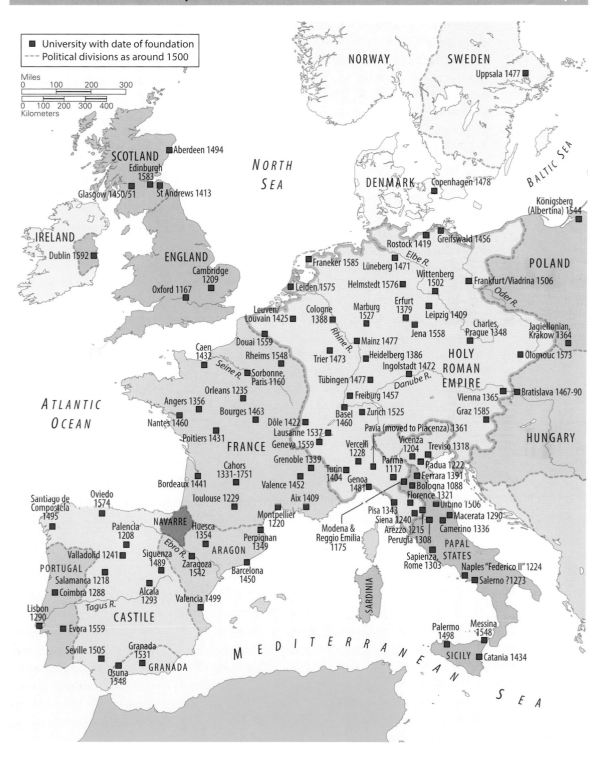

Legend:
- University with date of foundation
- Political divisions as around 1500

Miles: 0, 100, 200, 300
Kilometers: 0, 100, 200, 300, 400

NORWAY

SWEDEN

Uppsala 1477

NORTH SEA

BALTIC SEA

DENMARK

Copenhagen 1478

Königsberg (Albertina) 1544

SCOTLAND
Aberdeen 1494
Edinburgh 1583
Glasgow 1450/51
St Andrews 1413

Rostock 1419
Greifswald 1456

POLAND

IRELAND
Dublin 1592

ENGLAND
Cambridge 1209
Oxford 1167

Franeker 1585
Lüneberg 1471
Wittenberg 1502
Frankfurt/Viadrina 1506

Leiden 1575
Helmstedt 1576
Erfurt 1379
Leipzig 1409

Leuven/ Louvain 1425
Cologne 1388
Marburg 1527
Jena 1558
Charles, Prague 1348

Jagiellonian, Kraków 1364

Caen 1432
Douai 1559
Rheims 1548
Mainz 1477
Trier 1473
Heidelberg 1386
Ingolstadt 1472

Olomouc 1573

Orleans 1235
Sorbonne, Paris 1160
Tübingen 1477

HOLY ROMAN EMPIRE

Angers 1356
Bourges 1463
Freiburg 1457
Vienna 1365
Bratislava 1467-90

Nantes 1460
Dôle 1422
Basel 1460
Zurich 1525
Graz 1585

ATLANTIC OCEAN

Poitiers 1431
Lausanne 1537
Geneva 1559
Pavia (moved to Piacenza) 1361

FRANCE

Vercelli 1228
Vicenza 1204
Treviso 1318

HUNGARY

Cahors 1331-1751
Grenoble 1339
Turin 1404
Genoa 1481
Parma 1117
Padua 1222
Ferrara 1391

Bordeaux 1441
Valence 1452
Bologna 1088
Florence 1321

Toulouse 1229
Aix 1409
Urbino 1506

Santiago de Compostela 1495
Oviedo 1574
Montpellier 1220
Pisa 1343
Macerata 1290

Palencia 1208
NAVARRE
Huesca 1354
Perpignan 1349
Modena & Reggio Emilia 1175
Siena 1240
Arezzo 1215
Camerino 1336
Perugia 1308

Valladolid 1241
Siguenza 1489
Zaragoza 1542
ARAGON
PAPAL STATES

PORTUGAL
Salamanca 1218
Coimbra 1288
Alcala 1293
Barcelona 1450
Sapienza Rome 1303
Naples "Federico II" 1224

Lisbon 1290
Valencia 1499
Salerno ?1273

CASTILE
Evora 1559

Seville 1505
Granada 1531
GRANADA
Osuna 1548

SARDINIA

Palermo 1498
Messina 1548
SICILY
Catania 1434

MEDITERRANEAN SEA

Ebro R., Tagus R., Seine R., Rhine R., Elbe R., Oder R., Danube R.

The Waldensians

Around 1175 a merchant of Lyons, Peter Waldo (or Valdes, c. 1140–c. 1218), gave away his wealth to lead a life of poverty and preaching. He had vernacular translations made from the Latin New Testament and soon attracted many followers. But in little more than a decade what began as an enthusiastic popular movement had been branded as heresy.

Waldo's followers, the 'Waldensians', fled Lyons and started to organize as a church, spreading into two regions noted for unorthodox beliefs – Lombardy and Provence. By the end of the thirteenth century, though hounded by the newly strengthened Inquisition, the Waldensians had spread to much of Europe except Britain.

The greatest objection to the Waldensians, who began within the church, was that they ended up by rejecting that church. Unauthorized preaching from the Bible and the rejection of the mediating role of the clergy were major issues that gained them the reputation of heretics.

In the decades around 1400, in the Waldensians' main region, central and eastern Europe – particularly Bohemia, Moravia, Brandenburg, Pomerania, and Austria – they were widely persecuted by the Inquisition. During the fifteenth century Waldensians remained active in this region, exchanging ideas with the Hussites and helping create the charged atmosphere in which the great religious changes of the sixteenth century were to occur. In France the Waldensians continued to be harassed until the end of the Middle Ages, while in Italy they took refuge in the region of Piedmont, where they were attacked in 1488.

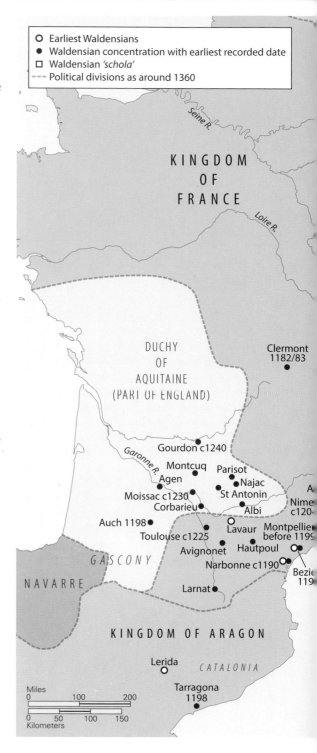

DISTRIBUTION OF THE WALDENSIANS

○ Earliest Waldensians
● Waldensian concentration with earliest recorded date
□ Waldensian 'schola'
--- Political divisions as around 1360

KINGDOM OF FRANCE

Seine R.

Loire R.

DUCHY OF AQUITAINE (PART OF ENGLAND)

Clermont 1182/83 ●

Garonne R.

Gourdon c1240 ●
Montcuq ●
Agen ●
Moissac c1230 ●
Corbarieu ●
Auch 1198 ●
Toulouse c1225 ●
Parisot ●
Najac ●
St Antonin ●
Albi ●
Lavaur ○
Montpellier before 119
Avignonet ●
Hautpoul ●
Narbonne c1190 ○
Larnat ●

A
Nime
c120

Bezie
119

GASCONY

NAVARRE

KINGDOM OF ARAGON

Lerida ○

CATALONIA

Tarragona 1198 ●

Miles
0   100   200

Kilometers
0   50   100   150

map 2

Mainz 1233

Main R.

Moselle R.

Metz 1200

Rhine R.

Toul

Strasbourg 1212

Regensburg c1262

Danube R.

Drosendorf

Nalb

Lengenfeld

Pupping

Stratzing

Langenlois

St Oswald

Anzbach

Neuhofen

St Christophen

Jonvelle 1218

Kammer

St Peter

Steyr

Ybbs

Ollersbach

Besançon
1248

H O L Y

R O M A N

Inn R.

E M P I R E

BURGUNDY

Rhône R.

SWISS
CONFEDERATION

Dongo

REPUBLIC
OF
VENICE

Gruaro

KINGDOM
OF
HUNGARY

yons
177

Vienne 1198

Legnano

Bergamo 1218

Milan before 1206

Verona
1199

Rhône R.

Valence c1235

Turin 1210

Pavia

Ronco

Cerea
before
1203

ontélimar

Pinerolo

Piacenza 1192/97

Po R.

nols

Embrun 1198

Modena

Faenza
1206

SERBIAN
PRINCIPALITIES

Bollène

REPUBLIC OF GENUA

Genoa

Orange

Sisteron

Florence 1206

A D R I A T I C

Carpentras

Avignon

PROVENCE

REPUBLIC
OF
FLORENCE

PAPAL

S T A T E S

S E A

Arles 1198

Aix 1198

ues-Vives
1204

REPUBLIC
OF
GENOA

Tiber

E D I T E R R A N E A N   S E A

Rome
1179

K I N G D O M

O F

N A P L E S

Important in preparing the way for the Reformation was the rise in northern Europe of a movement known as the *Devotio Moderna* ('the modern way of serving God'), a spiritual revival that began within the Catholic Church in the late fourteenth century, strongly emphasizing personal devotion and social involvement, especially in education.

Geert Groote (1340–84), from Deventer in the Netherlands, who had studied at Paris, had a religious experience in 1374 that led him to devote himself to practical piety. In his house at Deventer he gathered a community of poor women to live the common life together, without taking the vows of a convent.

Jan van Ruysbroeck (1293–1381), a Flemish mystic, and Florens Radewijns (c. 1350–1400), an ordained priest with organizing ability who had studied at Prague, both associated with Groote, who now founded a semi-monastic community of men, both lay and clergy, which now became known as the Brethren of the Common Life (Latin, *Fratres Vitae Communis*). When Groote died of plague, Radewijns took over leadership of this movement. They observed the threefold rule of poverty, chastity, and obedience, but were not bound by a formal vow. Any member was free to leave the brotherhood and return to secular life if he wished. In 1387 Radewijns founded the group's most influential house, at Windesheim, near Zwolle, and members became Augustinian canons, with constitutions approved by Pope Boniface IX in 1395. A few years later they combined with other houses in the Low Countries to form the 'Congregation of Windesheim'.

The members dedicated themselves to education and to spiritual discipline, renouncing the world. To support their community, they busied themselves with book-production: writing, copying manuscripts, binding, and marketing, and – with the advent of printing – operating their own press. In time the movement spread and during the fifteenth century the Windesheim Canons set up communities in Germany and Switzerland.

Many Brethren of the Common Life and those educated by them left their mark on the Christian world. Foremost of these were the philosopher and theologian Nicholas of Cusa (1401–64) and Desiderius Erasmus (1466–1536). Gabriel Biel (c. 1420–95), the philosopher known as 'the last German scholastic', and the humanist Rodolphus Agricola (1444–85) were both members of the community; the best elements of scholasticism and humanism co-existed in the *Devotio Moderna*. Perhaps the figure who best sums up the *Devotio Moderna* is Thomas Haemerken (c. 1380–1471), better known as Thomas à Kempis, author of *The Imitation of Christ*, the most popular devotional handbook of the Middle Ages.

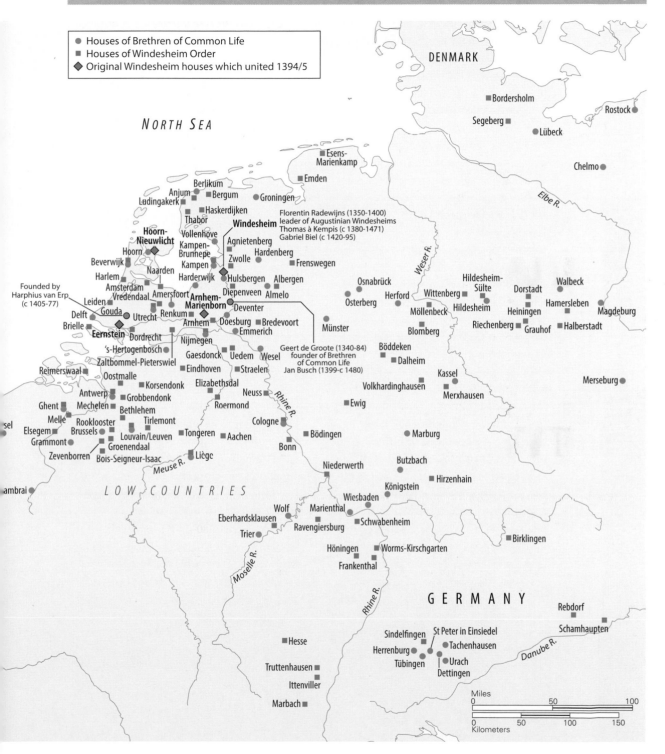

Houses of Brethren of Common Life
Houses of Windesheim Order
Original Windesheim houses which united 1394/5

DENMARK

Bordersholm

Segeberg

Rostock

Lübeck

Chelmo

NORTH SEA

Esens-Marienkamp

Emden

Berlikum

Anjum
Ludingakerk

Bergum

Groningen

Haskerdijken

Thabor

Windesheim

Florentin Radewijns (1350-1400) leader of Augustinian Windesheims
Thomas à Kempis (c 1380-1471)
Gabriel Biel (c 1420-95)

Hoorn-Nieuwlicht

Vollenhove

Agnietenberg

Kampen-Brunnepe

Hardenberg

Beverwijk

Zwolle

Frenswegen

Hoorn

Kampen

Harlem

Naarden

Harderwijk

Hulsbergen

Albergen

Osnabrück

Hildesheim-Sülte

Dorstadt

Walbeck

Amsterdam

Diepenveen

Almelo

Herford

Wittenberg

Hildesheim

Hamersleben

Founded by Harphius van Erp (c 1405-77)

Leiden

Vredendaal

Amersfoort

Arnhem-Marienborn

Deventer

Osterberg

Möllenbeck

Heiningen

Magdeburg

Delft

Gouda

Utrecht

Renkum

Doesburg

Bredevoort

Münster

Riechenberg

Grauhof

Halberstadt

Brielle

Eernstein

Dordrecht

Arnhem

Emmerich

Blomberg

Nijmegen

's-Hertogenbosch

Geert de Groote (1340-84) founder of Brethren of Common Life
Jan Busch (1399-c 1480)

Böddeken

Reimerswaal

Zaltbommel-Pieterswiel

Gaesdonck

Uedem

Wesel

Dalheim

Kassel

Merseburg

Oostmalle

Eindhoven

Straelen

Volkhardinghausen

Merxhausen

Antwerp

Korsendonk

Elizabethsdal

Neuss

Ewig

Ghent

Mechelen

Grobbendonk

Roermond

Bethlehem

Tirlemont

Cologne

Melle

Rooklooster

Tongeren

Aachen

Bödingen

Marburg

Elsegem

Brussels

Louvain/Leuven

Bonn

Grammont

Groenendaal

Butzbach

Zevenborren

Bois-Seigneur-Isaac

Liège

Niederwerth

Hirzenhain

Meuse R.

LOW COUNTRIES

Königstein

Wiesbaden

Wolf

Marienthal

Cambrai

Eberhardsklausen

Ravengiersburg

Schwabenheim

Trier

Birklingen

Höningen

Worms-Kirschgarten

Frankenthal

GERMANY

Rebdorf

Schamhaupten

Hesse

Sindelfingen

St Peter in Einsiedel

Herrenburg

Tachenhausen

Truttenhausen

Tübingen

Urach

Dettingen

Danube R.

Ittenviller

Marbach

Miles
0   50   100

0   50   100   150
Kilometers

Elbe R.

Weser R.

Rhine R.

Rhine R.

Moselle R.

The Great Schism

Crisis of the Papacy

The thirteenth century ended with the election and unheard-of abdication of Pope Celestine V in 1294. This threw the first pope of the fourteenth century, Boniface VIII (1294–1303), under a cloud of uncertainty. Papal and royal policies soon came into conflict; undignified squabbles recurred till the end of the Middle Ages.

Boniface's bull *Clericis laicos* (1296) limited the power of kings to tax their clergy while *Unam sanctam* (1302) epitomized extreme papal claims. Philip the Fair of France (r. 1285–1314) attacked the pope, who escaped from Anagni, Italy, to Rome, but died there shortly after. Political instability in Italy and the Papal States now rendered the papal seat in Rome untenable.

Under continued French pressure, the Archbishop of Bordeaux was elected Pope Clement V (1305–14). Clement, from Gascony, south-west France, never went to Rome, and chose Avignon, southern France, as his residence, thus becoming the first pope to live under the 'Babylonian Captivity of the Papacy' (1309–78). For most of the fourteenth century, no pope lived in Rome: a divorce between the head of Western Christendom and the Holy City that caused great scandal and unrest.

Clement's successor John XXII (1316–34) saw the papacy more in administrative than spiritual terms, while Benedict XII (1334–42) and Clement VI (1342–52) supported France against the English during the Hundred Years' War, the latter spending lavishly on pomp and ceremony and openly promoting members of his own family. By the time of Innocent VI (1352–62), pressure was growing on the popes to return to Rome. Innocent's successor, Urban V (1362–70) did return to Rome in 1367, but then appointed several French cardinals and in 1370 returned to Avignon. Gregory XI (1370–78) left Avignon finally in 1376, entering Rome in 1377. The papacy had at last returned to the Eternal City.

Great Schism

Following the death of Gregory XI, angry crowds demanded an Italian pope. The cardinals elected Urban VI (1378–89), who proved too much a dictator. Citing disorderly behaviour at his election as an excuse, some cardinals elected another pope, Clement VII (1378–94). After armed battles between forces of the rival popes, Clement VII retired to Avignon in 1381, beginning the 'Great Schism', a split of the government of the church that had both political and religious repercussions. Italy, the Holy Roman Empire, Scandinavia, Hungary, and England supported Urban VI of Rome; France, Spain, and Scotland supported Clement VII in Avignon. The problem continued after Clement's death, with parallel elections in Rome and Avignon continuing into the next century.

At length, rival colleges of cardinals in Rome and Avignon began to discuss ways of ending the Schism. Since neither pope would give way, some cardinals called a council at Pisa in 1409. Both popes refused to attend, so the cardinals deposed them and elected instead Alexander V (1409–10). Neither the Avignon nor the Roman pope recognized him, resulting in three popes where there had been two. Not until the Council of Constance (1414–17) was the split finally healed, when Martin V was acknowledged by nearly all as the sole and rightful pope.

NORWAY

SCOTLAND

NORTH SEA

DENMARK

BALTIC SEA

TEUTONIC KNIGHTS

IRELAND

WALES

ENGLAND

London

CALAIS

FLANDERS

PONTHIEU

Aachen

Rhine R.

Mainz

HOLY
ROMAN
EMPIRE

Oder R.

POLAND

Prague

Paris

Danube R.

ATLANTIC
OCEAN

FRANCE

Bordeaux

ENGLISH
GASCONY

Avignon

HUNGARY

NAVARRE

PAPAL
STATES

ADRIATIC SEA

OTTOMAN
EMPIRE
(MUSLIM MINORITY)

ARAGON

SARDINIA

Rome

NAPLES

PORTUGAL

CASTILE

Toledo

GRANADA

SICILY

MEDITERRANEAN SEA

Legend:
- Allegiance to Rome
- Allegiance to Avignon
- Neutral
- Changed allegiance
- Greek Orthodox
- Muslim
- — Holy Roman Empire boundary

1378: French cardinals
elect antipope Clement VII,
causing the Great Schism
Popes:
Clement V (1305-14)
John XXII (1316-34)
Benedict XII (1334-42)
Clement VI (1342-52)
Innocent VI (1352-62)
Urban V (1362-70) - in Rome 1367-1370;
returned to Avignon 1370
Gregory XI (1370-78);
left Avignon for Rome September 1376
Antipopes:
Clement VII (1378-94)
Benedict XIII (1394-1423);
expelled from Avignon on 1403

1378: Pope Urban VI
is elected under Italian
pressure, ending the
'Babylonian Captivity'
Popes:
Boniface VIII (1294-1303)
Benedict XI (1303-4)
Urban VI (1378-89)
Boniface IX (1389-1404)

Miles
0   100   200   300

0   100 200   400
Kilometers

Wyclif and the Lollards

John Wyclif (c. 1320–84), a leading philosopher at Oxford University, offended the church by supporting the government's right to seize the property of corrupt clergymen. His views were condemned by the pope in 1377, but influential friends protected him. Wyclif began to extend his anti-clerical views and to attack central doctrines of the medieval church, in particular transubstantiation. He wrote: 'no man is so rude a scholar but that he may learn the words of the Gospel ….'

A group of followers arose around Wyclif at Oxford, attracted by his energetic preaching. He was gradually deserted by his friends in high places, and the church authorities were able to force Wyclif and his followers out of Oxford. In 1382, a sick man, he went to live at Lutterworth, in the English Midlands, initiating a vernacular Bible translation by Nicholas Hereford (d. 1420): the *Wyclif Bible*. His followers spread to Leicestershire and became known as 'Lollards' – possibly meaning 'mumbler'. By 1395 the Lollards had developed into an organized group, with their own ministers and popular support.

The Lollards stood for many of the ideas set out by Wyclif, believing the main task of a priest was to preach, and that the Bible should be available to all in their own language. However it is unclear how far Wyclif's views constituted a 'premature Reformation'. From the beginning of the fifteenth century, the Lollards were suppressed, particularly when their protest became linked to political unrest.

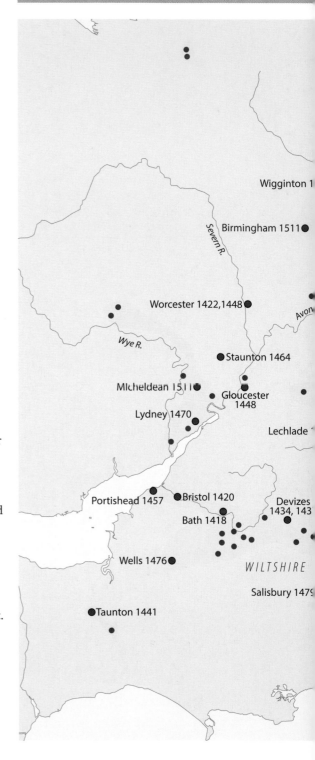

DISTRIBUTION OF THE LOLLARDS

Wigginton 1
Birmingham 1511
Severn R.
Worcester 1422,1448
Avon
Wye R.
Staunton 1464
Micheldean 1511
Gloucester 1448
Lydney 1470
Lechlade
Portishead 1457
Bristol 1420
Devizes 1434, 143
Bath 1418
Wells 1476
WILTSHIRE
Salisbury 1479
Taunton 1441

map 5

Heretics prosecuted, with date
Lollards and other heretics active

NORTH SEA

DERBYSHIRE

...nbourne 1488
Derby
Aston
Loughborough
Leicester 1511
Coventry 1424-25
Market Harborough
Corby 1417
Daventry
Banbury

Creake 1428
King's Lynn 1428
Thorpe 1428
Norwich 1428, 1510
Wymondham 1428

EAST ANGLIA

Somersham 1457
Mildenhall
Chesterton 1457
Cambridge 1457
Bury St Edmunds 1428
Eye 1428
Framlingham 1428
Leiston 1428
Ipswich 1428, 1521

...ford ...21
OXFORDSHIRE
Witney 1521
Kidlington 1416
Dunstable
Thame 1464
Oxford
Earingdon 1499
Wallingford 1443
...ngerford 1505
Henley 1462
Reading 1416
Newbury 1491
Windsor 1502

Hitchin
St Albans 1427
Barnet 1427
Amersham 1646
Waltham Abbey 1439, 1513
London 1415

Ware 1477, 1521
Colchester 1428
Chelmsford 1430, 1521
Maldon 1430

Thames R.

Strood 1436
Rochester 1425
West Malling 1425
Maidstone 1495
Canterbury 1469
Ashford 1511
KENT
Tonbridge 1496
Dover
Tenterden 1422
Romney 1425

Farnham 1440
...chester 1428
Rogate 1470
SUSSEX

ENGLISH CHANNEL

Trent R.
Ouse R.

Miles
0 10 20 30 40 50

0 10 20 30 40 50
Kilometers

WYCLIF AND THE LOLLARDS   33

Jan Hus and the Hussites

The marriage of Richard II of England to Anne of Bohemia in 1382 resulted in links between both countries and in some of Wyclif's writings reaching Bohemia. Wyclif's attacks on the church resonated with the discontents of Jan Hus (c. 1369–1415), who taught at the Charles University in Prague, and with other Czech churchmen. Hus took up the theme of church reform in sermons at the Bethlehem Chapel, Prague, that soon became hugely popular in the city and with the Czech nobility. His views merged with an assertion of Czech identity against German-speakers in the Bohemian church and nation and found support throughout society.

Under a safe-conduct from the Holy Roman Emperor, Hus was summoned to the church's General Council at Constance in 1414 to explain his acts of rebellion, but the council tried him for heresy regardless. Hus was burned at the stake in 1415, condemned by the council and the Emperor. Bohemia exploded in anger; within five years Czech rebels had established a Hussite Church in Bohemia, independent of Rome, and soon more radical elements began to challenge the secular hierarchy as well as the church. Decades of vicious civil war followed, alongside unsuccessful attempts by surrounding states to destroy the revolution.

The pope invoked five failed crusades against the Hussites, and rebellion spread to Austria, Slovakia, Silesia, Bavaria, and even the Baltic.

An independent Hussite church emerged, partially recognized by Rome. Unlike the Roman church, it used the Czech language in worship, and insisted that the people receive both bread *and* wine at the Eucharist. From this reception 'in both kinds' or 'species' (*sub utraque specie*), the Hussite movement derived its name 'Utraquism'. In the absence of a native episcopate, the church was effectively in the hands of the aristocracy and of the leaders in major cities – a characteristic of the 'official' Reformations of the next century.

More radical Hussites, the Union of Bohemian Brethren (*Unitas Fratrum*), separated from the Utraquists in 1457. Inspired by the south Bohemian writer Petr Chelcicky (c. 1390–c.1460), and invoking New Testament Christianity, they condemned all types of violence, including political repression, capital punishment, military service, and the swearing of oaths to earthly authorities, and rejected the idea of a separate priesthood and transubstantiation – all doctrines that re-emerged during the Reformation.

Jan Hus (c. 1369–1415),
Czech reformer and martyr.

DENMARK

BALTIC SEA

Bohemia
Hungary
Hussite region
Holy Roman Empire boundary
Hussite campaign
Significant battle

Gdansk

TEUTONIC KNIGHTS

POMERANIA

BRANDENBURG

Elbe R.

Berlin

Oder R.

Poznan

Varta R.

POLAND

Wisła R.

Magdeburg

Torgau

LUSATIA

Meissen

SAXONY

Dresden

SILESIA

Oder R.

Kraków

Ústí nad Labem 1426

Vítkov Hill 1420

Prague

Hradec Králové

Plzeň

Kutná Hora

Tachov 1427

Lipany 1434

Olomouc

uremberg

Domazlice (Taus) 1431

BOHEMIA

Tabor

MORAVIA

Brno

Trenčín

Kremnica

Kosice

Regensburg

České Budejovice

Banská Stiavnica

Danube R.

Passau

Trnava

HUNGARY

BAVARIA

Danube R.

Vienna

Bratislava

AUSTRIA

Esztergom

Buda

Miles
0   50   100
0   50   100   150
Kilometers

The Rise of Printing

The invention of printing – sometimes called Germany's chief contribution to the Renaissance – released a new energy into the story of books, scholarship, and education. In about 1445 Johannes Gutenberg (c. 1398–1468) started to experiment with movable metal type at Mainz, Germany. The first complete book known to have been printed in this way in the Christian world was the Bible (1456).

Until 1462 the new art remained a trade secret in Mainz, but that year the city was plundered and the printers dispersed. Within two decades printing presses were set up in Rome (1467), Paris (1470), Cracow (1474), and Westminster (1476). By the time Luther was born, in 1483, printing was well established throughout Europe.

The printing press was very important in the early spread of the Reformation. The writings of the first German reformers – Luther and Melanchthon – reached a wide public in printed form within weeks, and were soon being read in Paris and Rome. But even before the Reformation, printing helped to create a wider and more critical reading-public. It also met the new demand for reading material, with works such as the religious satires of Erasmus proving a big commercial success.

The invention of printing allowed the Bible to be circulated more widely than ever before. With this possibility came the desire of the Reformers to make what they regarded as the Word of God available to all people in their own language. This came at a time when it was unusual to write in the vernacular, and works such as the *Luther Bible* contributed greatly to the growth of the European languages.

THE EARLIEST PRINTING CENTRES IN EUROPE

map 7

NORWAY

SWEDEN

Stockholm 1483

BALTIC SEA

DENMARK

Odense 1482

Copenhagen 1493

Harlem 1483

ges 73-4

Lübeck 1474

Danzig 1499

Delft 477

Hamburg 1488

Deventer 1477

Elbe R.

Utrecht 1473

Gouda 1477

HOLY ROMAN EMPIRE

Oder R.

POLAND

Antwerp 1481

Louvain 1473-4

Cologne 1465

Leipzig 1480

Wroclaw 1475

ssels 75-6

Frankfurt 1478

Bamberg 1457

Kuttenberg 1489

Krakow 1473

Mainz 1452-3

Nuremberg 1469

Pilsen 1475

Brno 1486

Strasbourg 1460

Rhine R.

Augsburg 1468

Vienna 1482

Basel 1462

Munich 1482

Memmingen 1478

Danube R.

Buda 1473

Zurich 1479

HUNGARY

Geneva 1478

VENICE

ons 73

Milan 1470

Venice 1469

BLACK SEA

Bologna 1471

Florence 1471

OTTOMAN EMPIRE

PAPAL STATES

Rome 1467

Subiaco 1465

NAPLES

Constantinople 1488

Naples 1470

MEDITERRANEAN SEA

Major fifteenth-century printing centre, with date of first known printed book

Other fifteenth-century printing centres

Political boundaries in 1490

Miles
0   100   200   300

Kilometers
0   100   200   300   400

THE RISE OF PRINTING   37

The Italian Renaissance

'Renaissance' (re-birth) describes the revival of the values of classical Greek and Roman civilization in the arts, politics, and thinking that originated in Italy and spread over most of Western Europe. The Renaissance began with the revival of classical learning by scholars known as 'humanists'. A humanist was originally someone who taught Latin grammar, but later came to mean a student of Latin and Greek who not only read classical writings but shaped his life by what he read. Most of the early humanists professed Christianity, although Renaissance humanists also studied such non-Christian authors as Cicero and Plato.

The home of humanism was Italy, and the first known humanist Lovato Lovati (1241–1309), who not only read the Latin classics but tried to imitate their spirit. He discovered manuscripts of forgotten classics in the library of the abbey of Pomposa, precipitating a search for hidden treasures of antiquity that became one of the features of humanism.

Humanism came of age with the Italian Francesco Petrarca (or Petrarch, 1304–74), whose writings had a huge impact on European literature. Petrarch reacted against the Aristotelian form in which Christianity was presented by the medieval scholastics, polarizing Christian opinion between the old scholasticism and the new humanism. Petrarch bequeathed his successors the ideal of a world of classical values recaptured and displayed within the context of a restored Christianity.

Italy of the late fifteenth and early sixteenth centuries was divided into many minor – frequently warring – states. This period saw a great increase of Italian trade and the simultaneous growth of major banks and finance houses. During the Renaissance the various Italian states and cities competed for the services and prestige of major artists. The funds needed to sponsor these Renaissance artists and to beautify the increasingly ornate cities came partly from great mercantile families such as the Medicis of Florence (an early centre of Renaissance activity), the Sforzas of Milan, and the Estes of Ferrara.

Rome benefited hugely from the activities of Renaissance popes such as Julius II (r. 1503–13), Leo X (a Medici; r. 1513–21), and Clement VII (another Medici; r. 1523–34), all great patrons of art, architecture, and letters. Venice, with its vibrant commercial activities, was another major focus of Renaissance art and architecture.

The study of natural sciences also expanded during this period. Medicine flourished as the study of anatomy revealed some secrets of the body and the number of charitable hospitals multiplied. Astronomy also advanced, although astrology was still dominant. Italian mathematicians and scientists such as Paolo dal Pozzo Toscanelli (1397–1482), Luca Pacioli (1445–1517), and Leonardo da Vinci (1452–1519) led in their respective disciplines.

SWITZERLAND

AUSTRIA

--- Borders as around 1494

HUNGARY

BISHOPRIC OF TRENT

Giovanni Bellini – painter (c 1430–1516)
Giorgione – painter (c 1477–1510)
Titian – painter (1488–1576)
Palladio – architect (1508–80)
Veronese – painter (1528–88)
Tintoretto – painter (1518–94)
Giovanni Gabrielli – composer (c 1554/57– 1612)

Trent

Mantegna, painter (c 1431–1506)

DUCHY OF SAVOY

DUCHY OF MILAN

Milan

HOLY ROMAN EMPIRE

Verona

REPUBLIC OF VENICE

Padua

Venice

Mantua

MARQUISATE OF MONTFERRAT

Turin

COUNTY OF ASTI

Parma

MARQUISATE OF MANTUA

DUCHY OF FERRARA

MARQUISATE OF SALUZZO

REPUBLIC OF GENOA

Genoa

DUCHY OF MODENA

Ferrara

Bologna

Ravenna

OTTOMAN EMPIRE

REPUBLIC OF VENICE

FRANCE

REPUBLIC OF LUCCA

Correggio, painter (1489–1534)

SAN MARINO

Florence

Pisa

Arezzo

REPUBLIC OF FLORENCE

Urbino

Vasari – writer (1511–74)
Piero della Francesca, painter (c 1412–92)

Siena

REPUBLIC OF SIENA

Perugia

PAPAL STATES

ADRIATIC SEA

REPUBLIC OF RAGUSA

CORSICA (GENOA)

Brunelleschi – architect (1377–1446)
Ghiberti – sculptor (1378–1455)
Donatello – sculptor (1386–1466)
Botticelli – painter (1445–1510)
Leonardo da Vinci – painter (1452–1519)
Machiavelli – writer (1469–1527)
Bronzino – painter (1503–72)
Striggio – composer (c 1536–92)

Rome

KINGDOM OF NAPLES

Naples

TYRRHENIAN SEA

SARDINIA (ARAGON)

Bernini – sculptor (1598–1680)
Michelangelo – painter, architect, sculptor (1475–1564)
Raphael – painter (1483–1520)
Bramante – architect (1444–1514)
Palestrina – composer (1526–94)

Cagliari

MEDITERRANEAN SEA

Palermo

KINGDOM OF SCICILY (ARAGON)

Syracuse

Miles
0   50   100

0   50   100   150
Kilometers

THE ITALIAN RENAISSANCE   39

The Northern Renaissance

Before long the Renaissance spread from its country of origin and humanists began to appear widely in France, Germany, Holland, and England (c. 1500–1600) as well as in Spain and Portugal. The Renaissance came later to Northern Europe as it was further from the Mediterranean centres of trade and culture. The French invasion of Italy in 1494, and the ability of the newly invented printing press to spread ideas quickly and accurately, facilitated contact with the ideas of the Italian Renaissance. Moreover with the rise of towns and of national monarchies in France, England, Spain, and Portugal there was less resistance to the new ideas of the Renaissance.

Among leading humanists in France were Jacques Lefèvre d'Étaples (c. 1455–1536) and Guillaume Budé (1467–1540), whose precise, penetrating scholarship opened up the way for the Reformation in their country. In Germany Nicholas of Cusa (1401–64) was the leading speculative thinker, while Johann Reuchlin (1455–1522), author of *De Rudimentis Hebraicis* (1506), established the study of Hebrew in the West.

From the Netherlands came Erasmus of Rotterdam (1466–1536), the greatest of the humanists, for whose services kings and princes across Europe competed. His *Praise of Folly* satirized the follies and vices of his times, particularly those of the church, while further popularizing humanism. Erasmus remained a pious Christian, but favoured the idea that it was an individual's inner spirit, rather than outward shows of piety or empty rituals, which mattered.

In England the new learning flowered in such Christian humanists as John Colet (1467–1519), Dean of St Paul's, whose Oxford lectures on Paul's letters broke new ground. Sir Thomas More (1478–1535), author of *Utopia*, defended the study of classical Greek and Roman culture, claiming their knowledge and the study of the natural world could serve as a stairway to the study of the supernatural.

Fine art

The more religious nature of the Northern Renaissance is reflected in its art, where secular and mythological themes appear less frequently than in Italy. The German artist Albrecht Dürer (1471–1528) was strongly influenced by the efforts of the Italians and the ancient writer Vitruvius to find mathematical proportions for portraying the perfect figure.

Music

While the Renaissance saw the rebirth of classical learning and visual arts, musicians had no means of referring back to Greek and Roman music. Instead, Renaissance composers had creatively to innovate. Until this period most church music was solely vocal; however, during the Renaissance other instruments began to be employed alongside the choir – strings, brass, and small ensembles. The introduction of printed music ensured greater textual accuracy and uniformity and the rapid and widespread circulation of compositions, resulting in an increase in the early influence of composers upon one another.

A number of outstanding composers appeared in Burgundy, including Guillaume Dufay (c. 1400–74), Johannes Ockeghem (c. 1410/30–97), and Josquin des Prés (c. 1445–1521) – often referred to simply as 'Josquin' – who was regarded as the greatest

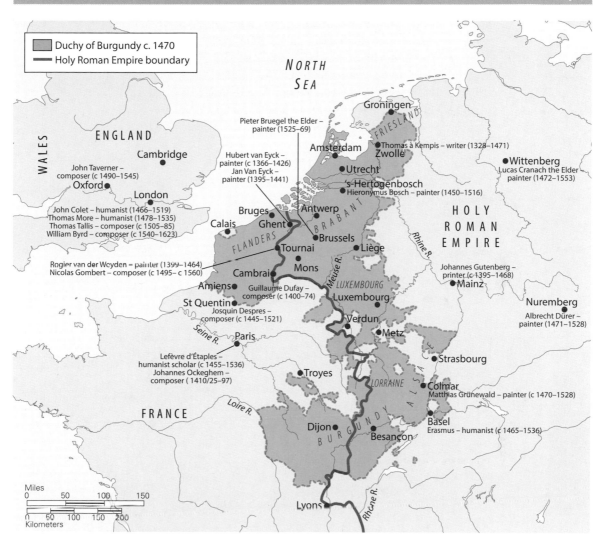

Duchy of Burgundy c. 1470
Holy Roman Empire boundary

NORTH SEA

Groningen

FRIESLAND

ENGLAND

WALES

Cambridge

Pieter Bruegel the Elder – painter (1525–69)

Amsterdam
Zwolle

Thomas à Kempis – writer (1328–1471)

Wittenberg
Lucas Cranach the Elder – painter (1472–1553)

Hubert van Eyck – painter (c 1366–1426)
Jan Van Eyck – painter (1395–1441)

John Taverner – composer (c 1490–1545)
Oxford

London

Utrecht

's-Hertogenbosch
Hieronymus Bosch – painter (1450–1516)

HOLY ROMAN EMPIRE

John Colet – humanist (1466–1519)
Thomas More – humanist (1478–1535)
Thomas Tallis – composer (c 1505–85)
William Byrd – composer (c 1540–1623)

Bruges
Calais
Ghent

Antwerp

BRABANT

Brussels

Rhine R.

Tournai
Liège

FLANDERS

Rogier van der Weyden – painter (1399–1464)
Nicolas Gombert – composer (c 1495–c 1560)

Cambrai
Mons

Meuse R.

Johannes Gutenberg – printer (c 1395–1468)
Mainz

LUXEMBOURG

Amiens
St Quentin

Guillaume Dufay – composer (c 1400–74)

Luxembourg

Nuremberg

Albrecht Dürer – painter (1471–1528)

Josquin Despres – composer (c 1445–1521)

Verdun

Metz

Seine R.
Paris

Strasbourg

Lefèvre d'Étaples – humanist scholar (c 1455–1536)
Johannes Ockeghem – composer (1410/25–97)

Troyes

LORRAINE

Colmar
Matthias Grünewald – painter (c 1470–1528)

ALSACE

FRANCE

Loire R.

BURGUNDY

Dijon
Besançon

Basel
Erasmus – humanist (c 1465–1536)

Miles
0   50   100   150

0   50   100   150   200
Kilometers

Lyons

Rhône R.

---

composer of his age. English Renaissance composers include John Taverner (c. 1490–c. 1548), remembered for his *Western Wind Mass*, Thomas Tallis (c. 1505–85), who navigated the politically treacherous waters of Tudor England, and William Byrd (1542/3–1623), 'father of British music' according to his admiring peers.

New universities

The fifteenth century also saw the foundation of many new and significant universities in Europe, among them Alcalá, Bordeaux, Louvain, St Andrews, Tübingen, and Uppsala. The University of Wittenberg, where Luther taught, was opened in 1502.

The Catholic Church in 1500

During the fifteenth century the papacy began to reap the results of centuries of compromise. The Great Schism saw two – even three – men claiming to be pope, and the Council of Constance staged a power struggle between bishops and pope, both events hindering papal government and harming the church's reputation in the eyes of the laity. The church continued to sell offices and indulgences, and remained the political plaything of princes and a useful source of income for second sons and the unscrupulous.

Criticism of clerical abuses had been widespread in Europe for centuries. But as society became more urbanized, better educated, and richer, the literate laity – often better educated than many of the priests who claimed to 'mediate the exclusive means of salvation' – increased criticism of the church and its clergy.

Yet in 1500 the Catholic Church stood outwardly undivided and virtually unchallenged. Its dioceses and archdioceses neatly divided up Western Europe; its bureaucracy was widely envied and its wealth was almost unmatched.

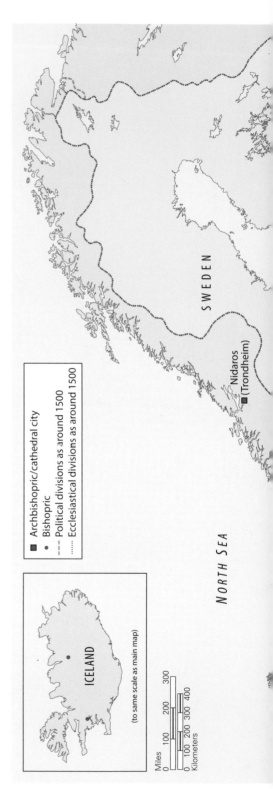

map 10

ECCLESIASTICAL DIVISIONS OF WESTERN EUROPE C. 1500

- ■ Archbishopric/cathedral city
- • Bishopric
- --- Political divisions as around 1500
- ⋯⋯ Ecclesiastical divisions as around 1500

SWEDEN

Nidaros (Trondheim)

NORTH SEA

ICELAND

(to same scale as main map)

Miles
0   100   200   300
0   100   200   300   400
Kilometers

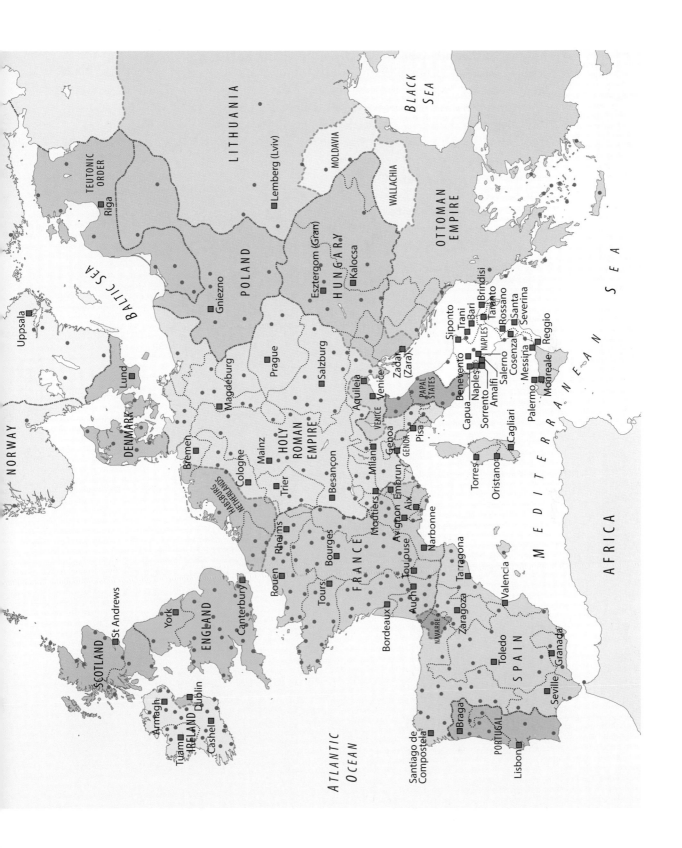

NORWAY

ATLANTIC OCEAN

Uppsala

BALTIC SEA

Lund

DENMARK

TEUTONIC ORDER

Riga

LITHUANIA

Lemberg (Lviv)

MOLDAVIA

BLACK SEA

WALLACHIA

OTTOMAN EMPIRE

POLAND

Gniezno

Esztergom (Gran)

HUNGARY

Kalocsa

Prague

Magdeburg

Salzburg

Bremen

Cologne

Mainz

HOLY ROMAN EMPIRE

Besançon

HABSBURG NETHERLANDS

Trier

Aquileia

Zadar (Zara)

VENICE

Venice

Genoa

GENOA

Pisa

PAPAL STATES

Siponto

Trani

Bari

Brindisi

Taranto

Rossano

Santa Severina

Reggio

Benevento

NAPLES

Capua

Naples

Sorrento

Amalfi

Salerno

Cosenza

Messina

Monreale

Palermo

MEDITERRANEAN SEA

Torres

Oristano

Cagliari

AFRICA

SCOTLAND

St Andrews

York

ENGLAND

Canterbury

Rouen

Rheims

Tours

Bourges

FRANCE

Moûtiers

Embrun

Avignon

Aix

Narbonne

Auch

Toulouse

Tarragona

Zaragoza

NAVARRE

Valencia

SPAIN

Toledo

Granada

Seville

Armagh

Tuam

IRELAND

Dublin

Cashel

Bordeaux

Braga

PORTUGAL

Lisbon

Santiago de Compostela

Portuguese Voyages of Discovery

China and India were vital to European trade in the Middle Ages. However the rise of the Ming dynasty (1368–1644) brought to an end Mongol control of China and southern Asia, closing off access to much of Asia for European merchants. At around the same time, the growth of Muslim power in the Middle East following the collapse of the Crusader kingdoms made land travel to India increasingly uncertain and hazardous. These changes helped stimulate sustained attempts by Europeans to reach India by sea.

In the fifteenth century, Portuguese and Spanish explorers made a series of exploratory voyages, later emulated by sailors from the maritime states of Genoa and Venice. In 1415, the Portuguese captured Ceuta, Morocco, and subsequently embarked on the progressive discovery of the West African coast. Iberian ships driven off these coasts discovered Atlantic islands such as Madeira, the Azores, and the Cape Verde Islands, which were then explored and colonized.

As Governor of the Order of Christ, the Portuguese Prince Henry the Navigator (1394–1460) funnelled much of this organization's wealth into scientific, commercial, and religious expeditions, with the ultimate aim of circumnavigating Africa. In 1434 a ship dispatched by Prince Henry passed the much-feared Cape Bojador, at that time regarded as the boundary of the knowable world. Having rounded this cape after a decade of trying, Henry's caravels reached the Senegal River in 1436 and Cape Blanc, at the southern limits of the Sahara Desert, in 1441. In 1444 one of his captains landed the first boatload of African slaves in Portugal, an ominous precedent. Progressing gradually further south, Portuguese sailors rounded Cape Verde in 1445, reaching Sierra Leone in 1457, the Gold Coast in 1471, and the Congo River in 1482. In 1490 Portuguese explorers worked their way up the river and converted to Christianity the king of the Kongo Empire.

The Church of our Lady of the Immaculate Conception, Goa, founded in 1540.

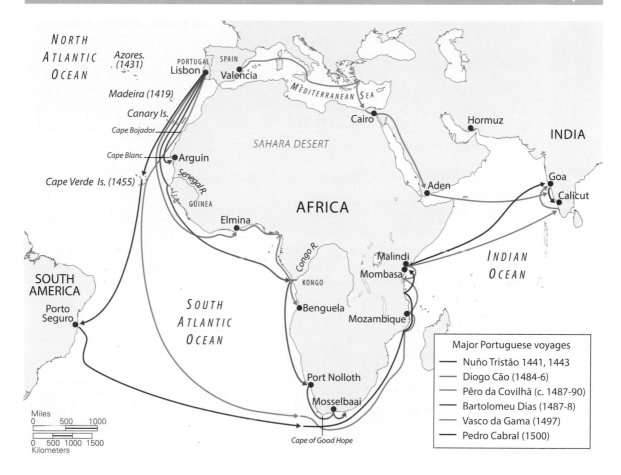

Major Portuguese voyages

— Nuño Tristão 1441, 1443
— Diogo Cão (1484-6)
— Pêro da Covilhã (c. 1487-90)
— Bartolomeu Dias (1487-8)
— Vasco da Gama (1497)
— Pedro Cabral (1500)

Dias and da Gama

Meanwhile Portuguese sailors continued to press southward. The daring voyage of Bartolomeu Dias (c. 1451–1500), who in 1488 rounded the Cape of Good Hope on the southern tip of Africa, disproved the long-held belief that India was inaccessible from the Atlantic Ocean. Finally in 1497 Vasco da Gama (c. 1460s–1524), having rounded the Cape, continued along the coast of East Africa and with the help of a pilot sailed across the Indian Ocean, reaching Calicut in 1498.

The Portuguese capital, Lisbon, now became a major trading centre with the East. Another outstanding seaman, Afonso de Albuquerque (c. 1453–1515), laid the basis of empire, taking Goa in India in 1510, Malacca in 1511, and Hormuz on the Horn of Arabia in 1515. These conquests evolved into a network of strategic Portuguese trading ports rather than colonies, since the Portuguese had neither the men nor the resources required to establish a colonial empire.

Spain Explores the West

Jealous of Portugal's discoveries, in 1492 Queen Isabella of Spain sponsored Christopher Columbus, a Genoese, to reach the East by sailing west. Having encountered indigenous brown-skinned people in what are now the Bahamas, Cuba, and Santo Domingo, he returned to report discovery of the 'Indies'. This opened up the 'new world' to Spanish conquest.

With Spain and Portugal both committed to exploration of the Americas, lines of demarcation were needed. The Treaty of Tordesillas (1494) was agreed with the complaisant Spanish Pope Alexander VI (r. 1492–1503), intended to divide off a Portuguese zone of influence in Africa and the East from the Spanish westerly explorations. The Portuguese managed to push the agreed line slightly west – on the grounds that their ships were often forced to sail far out into the Atlantic to catch favourable winds – which subsequently gave them rights to the as yet undiscovered territories of Brazil.

The initial Spanish campaigns of conquest in the New World were swift and bloody, and the lengthy process of exploitation was equally destructive. War, ill treatment, and hard, unfamiliar work all took a toll on the indigenous people; but most deadly were European diseases, against which they had no immunity. The indigenous population of central Mexico, estimated at 25 million in 1521, fell to 16 million by 1532 and a mere 2.6 million in 1568. To work the mines and fields – especially in the Caribbean – the Iberian invaders introduced black slaves, who were also decimated by disease, starvation, and cruelty.

From an early stage, missionaries accompanied the *conquistadores*, and a few priests, such as Bartolomé de Las Casas (1474–1560), attempted to protect the slaves and native Indians from cruelty and early death. But such efforts were largely thwarted.

Between 1529 and 1556 Charles V granted the Augsburg banking firm of Welser the rights to exploit the Chibcha Indian Empire – Venezuela and New Granada – while Francisco Pizarro (c. 1471–1541) conquered the Inca Empire and founded Lima, Peru. Hernán Cortés (1485–1547) conquered the Aztec Empire, founding Mexico City, after destroying the native capital, Tenochtitlan.

Other explorations

The French, British, Dutch, and Danish later made some incursions into the Caribbean and Central America, setting up their own colonies, while the Spanish pushed north into the areas now known as Florida, Texas, Arizona, New Mexico, and California. But France and the north European countries were slower to initiate voyages of discovery. In 1497 John Cabot (Giovanni Caboto, c. 1450 – c. 1499), a wealthy Italian merchant living in England, discovered Newfoundland while searching for Brazil. The following year he sailed along the coasts of Greenland, Labrador, Newfoundland, and New England before returning home. The first French explorations were made by Jacques Cartier up the St Lawrence River between 1534 and 1541.

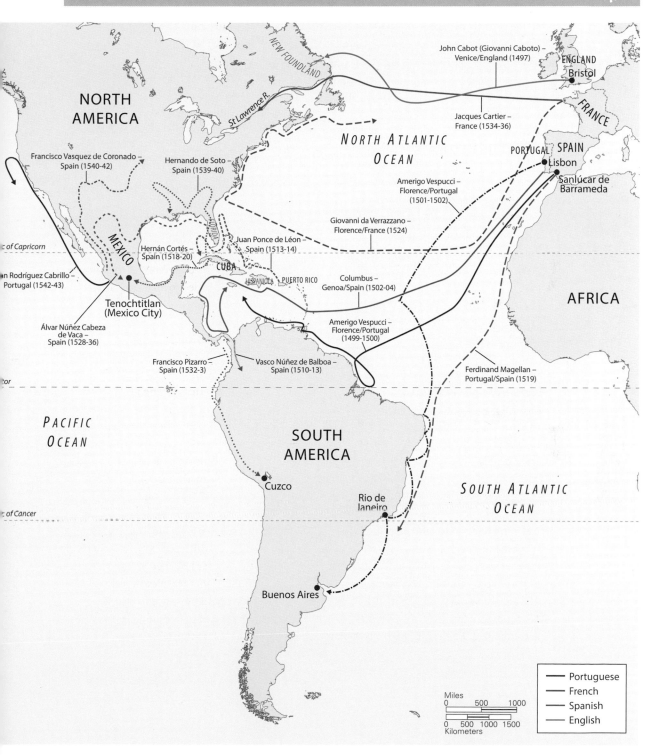

NORTH
AMERICA

St Lawrence R.

NEW FOUNDLAND

John Cabot (Giovanni Caboto) –
Venice/England (1497)

ENGLAND
Bristol

FRANCE

*NORTH ATLANTIC
OCEAN*

Jacques Cartier –
France (1534-36)

Francisco Vasquez de Coronado –
Spain (1540-42)

Hernando de Soto –
Spain (1539-40)

PORTUGAL SPAIN
Lisbon
Sanlúcar de
Barrameda

Amerigo Vespucci –
Florence/Portugal
(1501-1502)

Giovanni da Verrazzano –
Florence/France (1524)

of Capricorn

MEXICO

Hernán Cortés –
Spain (1518-20)

Juan Ponce de Léon –
Spain (1513-14)

CUBA

FLORIDA

HISPANIOLA　PUERTO RICO

Columbus –
Genoa/Spain (1502-04)

AFRICA

n Rodríguez Cabrillo –
Portugal (1542-43)

Tenochtitlan
(Mexico City)

Álvar Núñez Cabeza
de Vaca –
Spain (1528-36)

Amerigo Vespucci –
Florence/Portugal
(1499-1500)

Francisco Pizarro –
Spain (1532-3)

Vasco Núñez de Balboa –
Spain (1510-13)

Ferdinand Magellan –
Portugal/Spain (1519)

tor

*PACIFIC
OCEAN*

SOUTH
AMERICA

*SOUTH ATLANTIC
OCEAN*

Cuzco

Rio de
Janeiro

of Cancer

Buenos Aires

Miles
0　　500　　1000

0　500　1000 1500
Kilometers

—— Portuguese
—— French
—— Spanish
—— English

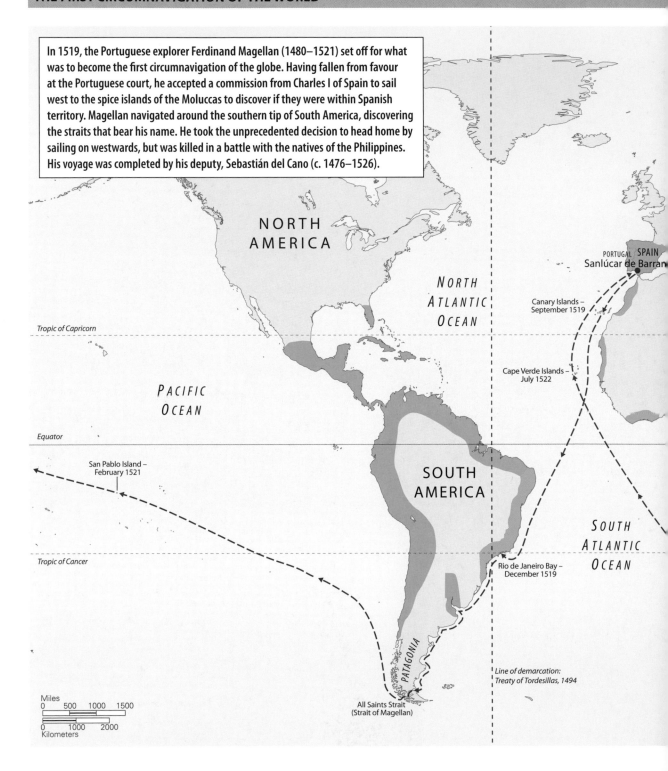

In 1519, the Portuguese explorer Ferdinand Magellan (1480–1521) set off for what was to become the first circumnavigation of the globe. Having fallen from favour at the Portuguese court, he accepted a commission from Charles I of Spain to sail west to the spice islands of the Moluccas to discover if they were within Spanish territory. Magellan navigated around the southern tip of South America, discovering the straits that bear his name. He took the unprecedented decision to head home by sailing on westwards, but was killed in a battle with the natives of the Philippines. His voyage was completed by his deputy, Sebastián del Cano (c. 1476–1526).

NORTH
AMERICA

NORTH
ATLANTIC
OCEAN

PORTUGAL SPAIN
Sanlúcar de Barran

Canary Islands –
September 1519

Tropic of Capricorn

Cape Verde Islands –
July 1522

PACIFIC
OCEAN

Equator

San Pablo Island –
February 1521

SOUTH
AMERICA

SOUTH
ATLANTIC
OCEAN

Tropic of Cancer

Rio de Janeiro Bay –
December 1519

Line of demarcation:
Treaty of Tordesillas, 1494

PATAGONIA

Miles
0   500   1000   1500

0   1000   2000
Kilometers

All Saints Strait
(Strait of Magellan)

map 13

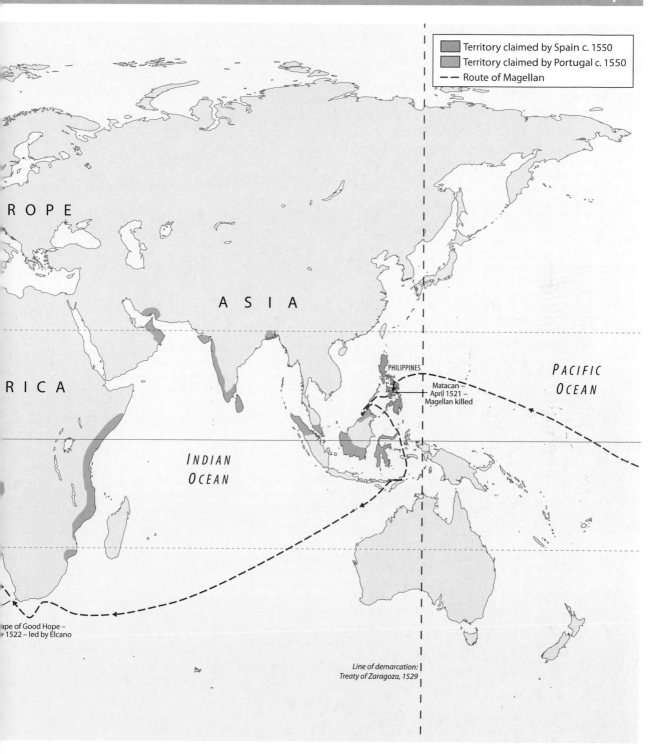

Territory claimed by Spain c. 1550
Territory claimed by Portugal c. 1550
- - - Route of Magellan

ROPE

ASIA

RICA

PACIFIC
OCEAN

PHILIPPINES

Matacan –
April 1521 –
Magellan killed

INDIAN
OCEAN

ape of Good Hope –
1522 – led by Elcano

Line of demarcation:
Treaty of Zaragoza, 1529

Part 2

Reformation

I am bound by the Scriptures I have quoted and my conscience is captive to the Word of God. I cannot and I will not recant anything, since it is neither safe nor right to go against conscience. May God help me.

MARTIN LUTHER

Charles V

Early sixteenth-century Western Europe was dominated by a trio of powerful and ambitious monarchs. Henry VIII (r. 1509–47), the first English king to be addressed as 'majesty', was courted by both the French king and the Holy Roman Emperor, and famously broke with the pope. Francis I (r. 1515–47) reinforced the absolutist claims of his immediate predecessors as King of France and unsuccessfully challenged Charles V for the title of Holy Roman Emperor. Meanwhile the Ottoman Turks under Suleiman the Magnificent (r. 1520–66) were looking enviously at the Christian north. The Sultan's armies took Belgrade in 1521 and defeated the Hungarian army at Mohács in 1526. However, Suleiman's siege of Vienna in 1529 was eventually raised, while his foray into Austria in 1532 was successfully resisted at Güns.

The third in this trio, the Holy Roman Emperor Charles V (r. 1519–56), attempted to maintain order, repel the Turks, heal the schism in the church caused by the Reformers, and defend and increase his hereditary holdings. As a descendant of Ferdinand of Aragon (r. 1479–1516) and Isabella of Castile (r. 1474–1504), he inherited the Spanish crown in 1516, taking the title Charles I. With the fall of Granada in 1492, the last of the Muslim Moors had been driven from the Iberian peninsula. Through Ferdinand and Isabella, Charles also received Sardinia, Sicily, the Kingdom of Naples, and the Balearic Islands. In addition, the newly colonized Spanish territories in North, Central, and South America poured wealth from the New World into his treasury.

Charles also inherited from his paternal grandmother, Mary of Burgundy (r. 1477–82), much of the Netherlands, Franche-Comté, and Luxembourg; and from his paternal grandfather, Maximilian I (r. 1508–16), the Habsburg lands of Germany. Shortly afterwards the Habsburgs also claimed the eastern flank of the Empire: Hungary, Bohemia, Moravia, and Silesia. In 1519 Charles was elected Holy Roman Emperor becoming, at least in name, sovereign of the central lands of Europe too.

However Charles' extensive holdings and ambitions did not allow him an easy rule. Charles and Francis I both laid claim to the Kingdom of Naples, Milan, Burgundy, Flanders, and Artois. There was also rivalry between the Pope and Charles, and it was papal policy that no power should control both Naples and Milan. The pope often backed Francis rather than Charles: Pope Leo X supported Francis over Charles in the imperial elections, and Pope Clement VII allied himself with the French king at a time when concerted action with Charles might otherwise have crushed the Reformation.

During the 1550s Charles gradually abdicated from parts of his empire. He gave Sicily, Naples, and Milan to his son Philip in 1554; he abdicated from the Netherlands in 1555; and from his Spanish Empire in 1556. Finally his brother Ferdinand succeeded as Holy Roman Emperor in 1558, shortly before Charles' death.

THE EMPIRE OF CHARLES V

EDINBURGH

NORTH SEA

DENMARK
Copenhagen

Danzig

IRELAND

ENGLAND

London

POLAND

HOLY
ROMAN
EMPIRE

LUSATIA

SILESIA

Elbe R.

Oder R.

Francis I and Charles V
both claim Artois
and Flanders

ARTOIS
Ghent
FLANDERS

Cologne

Mainz

Rhine R.

BOHEMIA

MORAVIA

1530; Lutherans present
Charles V with
Augsburg Confession

Danube R.

Vienna

HUNGARY

Seine R.
Paris

Augsburg

Vienna 1529

Duchy of Burgundy
claimed by
Francis and Charles

DUCHY
OF
BURGUNDY

COUNTY
OF
BURGUNDY

AUSTRIA

Budapest

ATLANTIC
OCEAN

Nantes

CHAROLAIS

FRANCE

Trent

VENICE

Mohacs 1526

Milan

Venice

1516 Charles proclaimed
King Charles I of Spain

Toulouse

Avignon

Genoa

Ottoman
Turks

Francis I and
Charles V both
claim Milan

Florence

PAPAL
STATES

ADRIATIC SEA

OTTOMAN
EMPIRE

NAVARRE

ARAGON

Barcelona

CORSICA

Rome

SPAIN

Madrid

Toledo

PORTUGAL

Tagus R.

SARDINIA

NAPLES

1519: Charles V crowned
Holy Roman Emperor
by the Pope

Naples

Francis I and Charles V
both claim Naples

Balearic Is.

sbon

Seville

Granada

MEDITERRANEAN SEA

SICILY

Algiers

Tunis

Oran

es
100   200

100 200 300
ometers

Inherited by Charles V
Gained by Charles V
Holy Roman Empire boundary
N.B. This does not include Charles V's overseas empire.

Martin Luther

Martin Luther (1483–1546) was born in Eisleben, a small mining town in north-east Germany, grew up in Mansfeld, and was educated in Eisenach, Magdeburg, and the University of Erfurt, where he studied law. In 1505 he joined a closed Augustinian friary in Erfurt, after having made a dramatic vow during a thunderstorm. Ordained in 1507, he studied theology and rose through the academic ranks at the university. Transferring to the new University of Wittenberg in 1511, he was linked with that institution for the rest of his life. In 1510–11 Luther visited Rome for his order, and was profoundly shocked by the corruption and extravagance he encountered in the papal city. In 1512 he became a doctor of theology and professor of biblical studies at Wittenberg.

After a long spiritual crisis, Luther rejected theology based on the inherited tradition, emphasizing instead the individual understanding and experience of Scripture, crucially believing justification not to be by works, but by faith alone. Luther's views became more widely known when he sent a letter to the bishops, including Albrecht, Bishop of Mainz, on 31 October 1517 and later (probably mid-November) posted his 95 Theses – intended for academic debate about the sale of indulgences and the church's material preoccupations – on the door of Wittenberg's Castle Church. Their effect was to undermine the basis of contemporary practice.

In December the Archbishop of Mainz complained to Rome about Luther. The latter refused to recant, travelled to Heidelberg in 1518 having prepared a set of theses for disputation before his Augustinian order, and was then examined by Cardinal Thomas Cajetan (1469–1534) in Augsburg. When he heard he might be arrested, Luther fled. In July 1519, during a disputation at Leipzig with his sharpest opponent Johann Eck (1486–1543), Luther denied the supremacy of the pope and the infallibility of church councils. Two years later he was excommunicated.

At the famous Diet of Worms in April 1521, standing before the Holy Roman Emperor in person, and fearing for his life, Luther again refused to recant. He was declared an outlaw, but kidnapped for his own protection by the sympathetic Elector Frederick of Saxony and taken to the Wartburg Castle. There he devoted his energies to translating the New Testament into German.

Since 1483 Saxony had been divided into two parts: Ernestine and Albertine, or Electoral and Ducal respectively. During his career as reformer, Luther was fortunate to live in Electoral Saxony, where the ruler, Elector Frederick the Wise (r. 1483–1525), despite remaining a Catholic, protected

Martin Luther (1483–1546).

ATLAS OF THE EUROPEAN REFORMATIONS

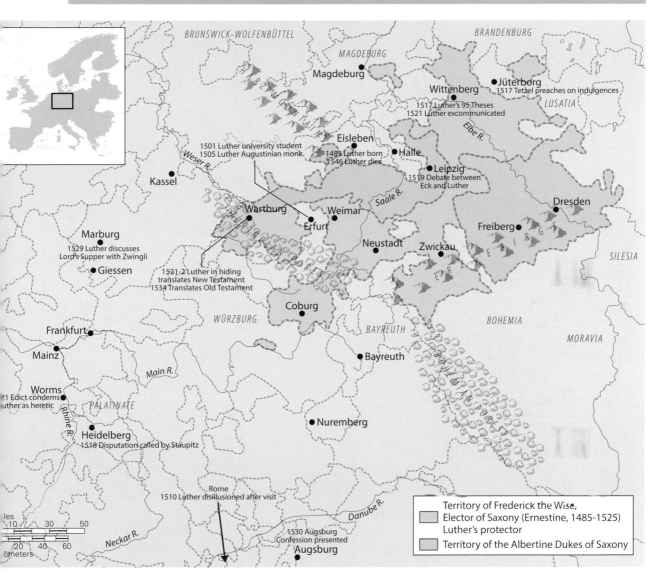

BRUNSWICK-WOLFENBÜTTEL

BRANDENBURG

MAGDEBURG

Magdeburg

Wittenberg
•Jüterborg
1517 Tetzel preaches on indulgences

LUSATIA

1517 Luther's 95 Theses
1521 Luther excommunicated

Elbe R.

Eisleben
1501 Luther university student
1505 Luther Augustinian monk

Weser R.

1483 Luther born   •Halle
1546 Luther dies

Kassel

•Leipzig
1519 Debate between
Eck and Luther

Dresden

Wartburg   Weimar
Freiberg

Erfurt

Marburg
1529 Luther discusses
Lord's Supper with Zwingli

Neustadt

Zwickau

SILESIA

•Giessen

1521-2 Luther in hiding
translates New Testament
1534 Translates Old Testament

Coburg

WÜRZBURG

BAYREUTH

BOHEMIA

MORAVIA

Frankfurt•

•Bayreuth

Mainz

Main R.

Worms
21 Edict condems
uther as heretic

PALATINATE

Rhine R.

•Nuremberg

Heidelberg
1518 Disputation called by Staupitz

Rome
1510 Luther disillusioned after visit

les
10   30   50

20   40   60
meters

Danube R.

Neckar R.

1530 Augsburg
Confession presented
Augsburg

Territory of Frederick the Wise,
Elector of Saxony (Ernestine, 1485-1525)
Luther's protector

Territory of the Albertine Dukes of Saxony

him when both Empire and Church turned against him. Ducal Saxony, on the other hand, was ruled by Duke George, a fierce opponent of Luther. The Leipzig debate took place in his territory.

In 1529 Luther travelled to Marburg for a colloquy with Zwingli and other reformers from Switzerland and south Germany; but the majority of his days were spent within the narrower limits of Saxony. The 'Luther Lands' are bounded by the Erzgebirge (Bohemian Massif) on the south-east, Electoral Saxony to the north-east, the Harz Mountains in the north-west, and the Thuringian Forest around the Wartburg in the south-west. No city in this region is more than 75 miles from Wittenberg.

The German Knights' War

Given the revolutionary nature of Lutheranism and the economic and political tensions of the time, it is not surprising that the Reformation soon became marked by violence and extremism. The German Knights' War of 1522–23, in which members of the lower nobility – some of them strong supporters of Luther – rebelled against the authorities in south-west Germany, was quickly crushed.

As medieval society began to crumble, the lesser nobility of the German states found themselves squeezed between powerful forces they could neither control nor moderate. Many depended upon dwindling payments in kind from their lands, a shortage of income made more acute by the spiralling inflation that followed the discovery and plundering of the New World. The increased authority of kings, together with the power and wealth of some princes of the church, further jeopardized the status, and excited the envy, of the knightly class. Their self-image had been flattered by the medieval code of chivalry and their role in the Crusades; now both their economic base and political power were declining rapidly.

Revolt

The knights rose in revolt under Franz von Sickingen (1481–1523) and Ulrich von Hutten (1488–1523). Both became adherents of the Lutheran cause, seeing in it an opportunity to recover the declining influence of the Christian nobility in the German nation. Sickingen, who had previously fought for the emperors Maximilian and Charles V, was sometimes called 'the last knight'. With Hutten, he proposed the unification of German-speaking lands and secularization of ecclesiastical principalities. Influenced by

The Sickingen Heights, in the Palatinate, Germany, near von Sickingen's town, Landstuhl.

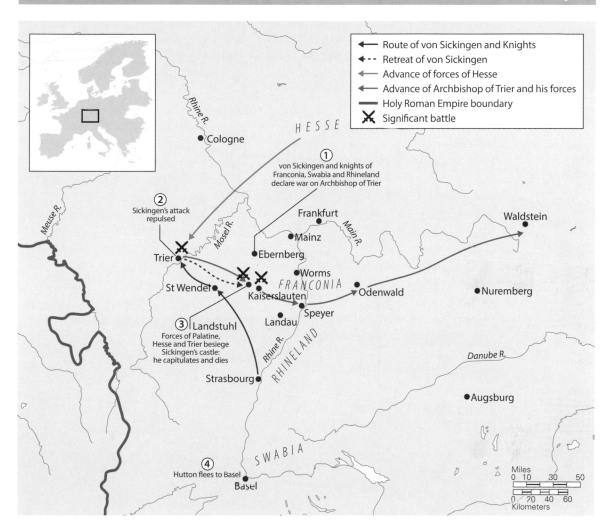

Route of von Sickingen and Knights
Retreat of von Sickingen
Advance of forces of Hesse
Advance of Archbishop of Trier and his forces
Holy Roman Empire boundary
Significant battle

HESSE

① von Sickingen and knights of Franconia, Swabia and Rhineland declare war on Archbishop of Trier

② Sickingen's attack repulsed

③ Landstuhl
Forces of Palatine, Hesse and Trier besiege Sickingen's castle: he capitulates and dies

④ Hutton flees to Basel

Cologne
Frankfurt
Mainz
Ebernberg
Trier
Worms
St Wendel
FRANCONIA
Kaiserslauten
Odenwald
Nuremberg
Speyer
Landau
Waldstein
Strasbourg
RHINELAND
Augsburg
Basel
SWABIA

Rhine R.
Meuse R.
Mosel R.
Main R.
Rhine R.
Danube R.

Miles
0 10   30   50
0 20   40   60
Kilometers

Hutten, Sickingen made his Rhineland estate, the Ebernburg, into a refuge for Lutheran sympathizers and a centre for Lutheran propaganda. He gave shelter to the reformers Martin Bucer and Johannes Oecolampadius, and even offered refuge to Luther following the Diet of Worms.

While Charles V was away in Spain, Sickingen summoned a gathering of knights and declared war on the Archbishop of Trier, a prominent opponent of Luther. His assault failed and he retreated to his supposedly unassailable stronghold at Landstuhl, where he was defeated and killed by an alliance of three German princes. Following Sickingen's defeat, Hutten fled to Basel, Switzerland.

The common refusal to pay church tithes during the revolt spread to the peasants and inspired them to refuse to pay the tithe – one of the factors that led to the Peasants' Revolt.

The Peasants' War

While Martin Luther was in protective custody at the Wartburg Castle, back in Wittenberg his colleague Andreas Karlstadt started to attack clerical celibacy and the ritual of the Mass. Also outsiders (the 'Zwickau prophets') arrived, claiming direct inspiration by the Holy Spirit and that the eucharistic bread and wine were symbols and in no sense the body and blood of Christ. Baptizing babies was also called into question. Luther soon intervened to bring matters back under his control.

But Luther's ideas and protest – particularly his emphasis on Christian freedom – were helping rapidly to produce socio-religious ferment throughout Germany. Significant numbers of clergy led attacks on the Mass; various towns introduced reforms; many nobles imposed religious change in their estates; and monks and nuns abandoned their vows.

Late in 1524 rural strikes and armed protests flared up across much of the country, escalating into the so-called Peasants' (or better 'Tenants") War, the biggest and most widespread popular uprising in Europe until the French Revolution of 1789. Similar protests had occurred previously, but this was far more extensive, representing the coming together of economic and social grievances with ideas derived from the Reformation. In German-speaking areas as widely scattered as Alsace, the fringes of the Alps, the borders of Bohemia, Hungary, and the kingdom of Poland there were strikes, disorder, and rebellions. Hostility was particularly aimed at clerical landlords. The first three of the Twelve Articles drawn up by the tenant farmers (*Bauern*) of Swabia called for the right to elect the parish priest, to use the tithe locally for the priest and poor, and for the end of serfdom.

Initially the Emperor was preoccupied with Italian wars against the French, but after gaining a decisive victory at the Battle of Pavia in February 1525 his forces, under Georg III, Truchsess von Waldburg-Zeil (also known as *Bauernjorg*, 1488–1531), turned north to Germany, where with the aid of local princes, such as Philip of Hesse and George of Saxony, they set about putting down the rebellion with bloody battles, torture, and mass killings.

Luther's room in the Wartburg Castle.

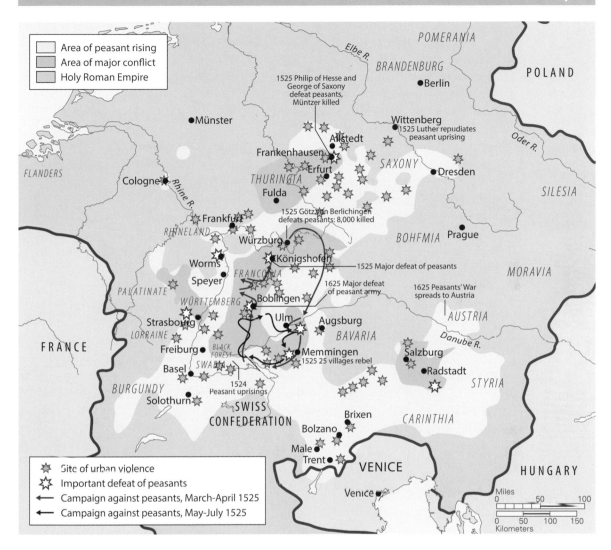

Luther responded to the Peasants' Revolt with an *Admonition to Peace* (April 1525) that laid the blame for the rebellion on princes, lords, and 'blind bishops, mad priests, and monks', but reminded the peasants that 'the governing authorities are instituted by God'. However after a perilous journey to negotiate with the rebels, Luther became convinced anarchy was unleashed and wrote *Against the Robbing and Murdering Hordes of Peasants*. This was published just days before the rebellion collapsed and appeared to justify the ensuing reign of terror by the Emperor and princes in which the final death toll may have reached 100,000. Luther, the champion of lay Christians, seemed to have turned himself into an apologist for state butchery.

The Radical Reformation

The Reformation progressed strongly in the Swiss city of Zurich. Following the logic of the prohibition in the Ten Commandments on 'making graven images', enthusiastic citizens began to destroy religious statues. Study of the New Testament led some to conclude that the apostles had baptized believing adults – not newborn babies. In accordance with this, in January 1525 a small group of Zurichers first baptized themselves and then others. Since all had been baptized as babies, opponents dubbed them 'Anabaptists', or re-baptizers. The Anabaptists did not regard this as re-baptism but as their first, since infant baptism was no baptism at all.

The Anabaptists soon won many converts, particularly in villages south and east of the city. When the Zurich Anabaptists were arrested most recanted, but in 1526 four were executed by drowning and the others expelled. Anabaptist membership was voluntary and groupings appeared, disappeared, and fluctuated. They were normally only a small minority, and three main strands can be detected.

An influential group of 'Swiss Brethren' met in 1527 near Lake Constance and agreed upon the 'Brotherly Union of a Number of Children of God Concerning Seven Articles'. They claimed adult baptism was mandatory, the Eucharist was a memorial ordinance, pastors were to be elected, and believers should separate themselves from society – taking no part in civic affairs and renouncing the use of force. They also refused to swear oaths. However although in Wittenberg Karlstadt had also questioned infant baptism, and Luther had ejected the enthusiastic Zwickau prophets, no links have been established between those radicals and the Swiss Anabaptists.

A second strand of the radical movement was focused on southern Germany, with Augsburg an early centre, led by Hans Denck (1495–1527) and a bookseller named Hans Hut (c. 1490–1527).

Eventually the Swiss and south German Anabaptists were driven to take refuge in the relative safety of Moravia. Led by Balthasar Hubmaier (c. 1485–1528), a refugee from Waldshut and Zurich, and Jakob Hutter (c. 1500–36), who brought his followers from Tyrol, the 'Hutterites' developed a communal lifestyle and in the third quarter of the sixteenth century possibly numbered 30,000. But soon Moravia ceased to be a safe haven and over the next two centuries survivors of these groups were driven from place to place in Eastern Europe until they found eventual refuge in North America.

The behaviour of a third stream – in north-west Europe – largely accounted for the paranoia concerning Anabaptists that came to dominate the sixteenth century. In the Low Countries the evangelist Melchior Hoffman (c. 1500–c. 1543) won many converts to a form of Anabaptist belief that expected the imminent arrival of God's final triumph. This region was under the direct rule of the Habsburgs, who initiated a merciless persecution of such 'heretics'. Their victims fled, finding refuge in the episcopal city of Münster, where reform was already in progress. By this time Hoffman was in prison in Strasbourg, but the 'Melchiorites' seized control of Münster and proclaimed the 'New Jerusalem'. Thousands from Friesland and nearby flocked to the city to be baptized and await the end of the age.

Münster

In April 1534, the Bishop of Münster joined forces with Lutheran nobles and cities to besiege the city, inside which radical steps were being taken to inaugurate the new

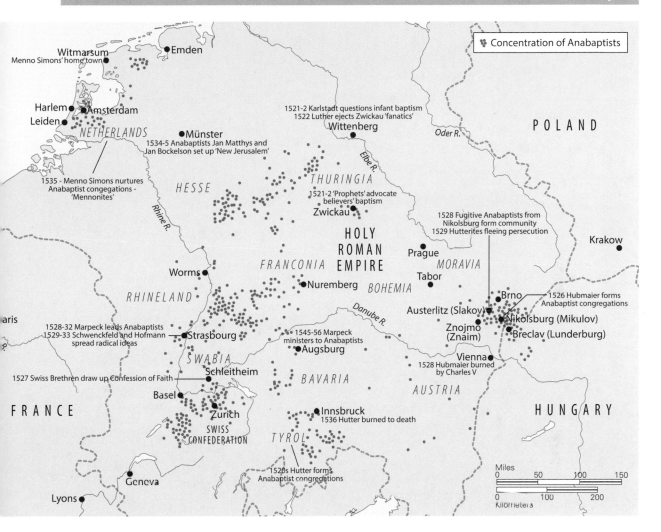

Concentration of Anabaptists

Witmarsum
Menno Simons' home town
Emden
Harlem
Leiden
Amsterdam
NETHERLANDS
Münster
1534-5 Anabaptists Jan Matthys and
Jan Bockelson set up 'New Jerusalem'
1535 - Menno Simons nurtures
Anabaptist congregations -
'Mennonites'
HESSE
Rhine R.
1521-2 Karlstadt questions infant baptism
1522 Luther ejects Zwickau 'fanatics'
Wittenberg
Oder R.
POLAND
THURINGIA
1521-2 'Prophets' advocate
believers' baptism
Zwickau
HOLY
ROMAN
EMPIRE
FRANCONIA
Worms
Nuremberg
Prague
MORAVIA
Tabor
BOHEMIA
Krakow
1528 Fugitive Anabaptists from
Nikolsburg form community
1529 Hutterites fleeing persecution
RHINELAND
1528-32 Marpeck leads Anabaptists
1529-33 Schwenckfeld and Hofmann
spread radical ideas
aris
Strasbourg
Danube R.
1545-56 Marpeck
ministers to Anabaptists
Augsburg
SWABIA
Schleitheim
1527 Swiss Brethren draw up Confession of Faith
Basel
FRANCE
Zurich
SWISS
CONFEDERATION
Austerlitz (Slakov)
Znojmo
(Znaim)
Brno
1526 Hubmaier forms
Anabaptist congregations
Nikolsburg (Mikulov)
Breclav (Lunderburg)
Vienna
1528 Hubmaier burned
by Charles V
BAVARIA
AUSTRIA
Innsbruck
1536 Hutter burned to death
HUNGARY
TYROL
1520s Hutter forms
Anabaptist congregations
Geneva
Lyons
Miles
0   50   100   150
0   100   200
Kilometers

society. Property was declared to be common
and polygamy made mandatory. The leaders,
headed by the tailor Jan Beukels – 'John of
Leiden' – lost all connection with reality.
He lived in luxury, took sixteen wives, and
proclaimed himself king of the world. In
1535 the city was betrayed to the bishop and
resistance collapsed in a bloodbath.

The fall of Münster marked the end of
militant Anabaptism – apart from the radical
sect of Zwaardgeesten ('sword-minded')
led by Jan van Batenburg (1495–1538) – as

a wave of persecution swept across Europe
and thousands were slaughtered. Of the
survivors, many turned to mysticism and
inner enlightenment. The largest group was
nurtured by the clandestine ministry of a
former country priest, Menno Simons (1496–
1561). These Mennonite communities –
quietist and pacifist – survived continual
Habsburg persecution and when the Dutch
Republic was set up later in the century
eventually achieved toleration.

The Ashkenazi Jews of northern Europe suffered frequent and widespread persecution during the Middle Ages. Jews were allowed by law to live only in restricted areas and work in prescribed businesses, such as money-lending to princes and merchants; hence the caricature of the Jew as extortionist and usurer. Although there had been major urban Jewish communities in German-speaking regions, many were expelled for allegedly poisoning wells or spreading plague – from Cologne in 1424, from Munich in 1442, and from Nuremberg in 1499.

A Catholic priest in Regensburg (Ratisbon), Balthasar Hübmaier (c. 1485–1528) preached a series of diatribes against the Jews that led to the burning of their synagogue and expulsion of the large Jewish community. In his later years, Martin Luther looked in disappointment at what he regarded as the partial failure and corruption of the Reformation. He had anticipated that the conversion of the Jews would accompany the restoration of a purified gospel. When this didn't happen, he turned against the Jews with some of his most scurrilous writing in the tract *Of the Jews and Their Lies*, where he argued that synagogues and Jewish schools should be burned, rabbis forbidden to teach, and Jewish religious books confiscated.

In a period of economic inflation, and against the background of the Peasants' War, the German Knights' War, the threat of Turkish invasion, the wars of religion, and recurring epidemics in the expanding cities, the frustrations and resentments of the masses during the sixteenth century found easy release in attacks on the Jews.

Inquisition

The Sephardic Jews of Spain were largely unaffected by the Christian reconquest of the Iberian peninsula and lived in established communities. However, growing political instability and condemnatory sermons by church leaders turned people against them.

In 1391 anti-Jewish violence in Seville spread to Castile and Aragon. Thousands of Jews chose to convert to Christianity and were labelled *marranos* ('swine'). By the middle of the fifteenth century they faced renewed hostility when the Spanish Inquisition questioned the genuineness of their new Christian faith, often using barbaric methods to root out crypto-Jews.

In 1492, after the capture of the Alhambra of Granada – the last bastion of Islam – Ferdinand and Isabella banished all Jews from Spain. Between 100,000 and 150,000 Jews departed, some across the border to Portugal, but most to North Africa or Ottoman Turkey. Some found refuge in the Papal States, where the Inquisition was less severe than in Spain, and where they were to influence the thinking of some north Italian Humanists and radical reformers, among whom Anti-Trinitarianism frequently appeared.

The Counter-Reformation later brought renewed suffering to the Jews of Catholic Europe. The papal bull *Vices eius nos* (1577) required 100 male and 50 female Jews in the papal states to attend conversionist sermons every Saturday afternoon (the Jewish Sabbath) in a church near the ghetto, often delivered by renegade Jews such as the medical doctor Vitale de' Medici (previously the rabbi Jehiel da Pesaro), a custom that continued in Italy and France until the French Revolution.

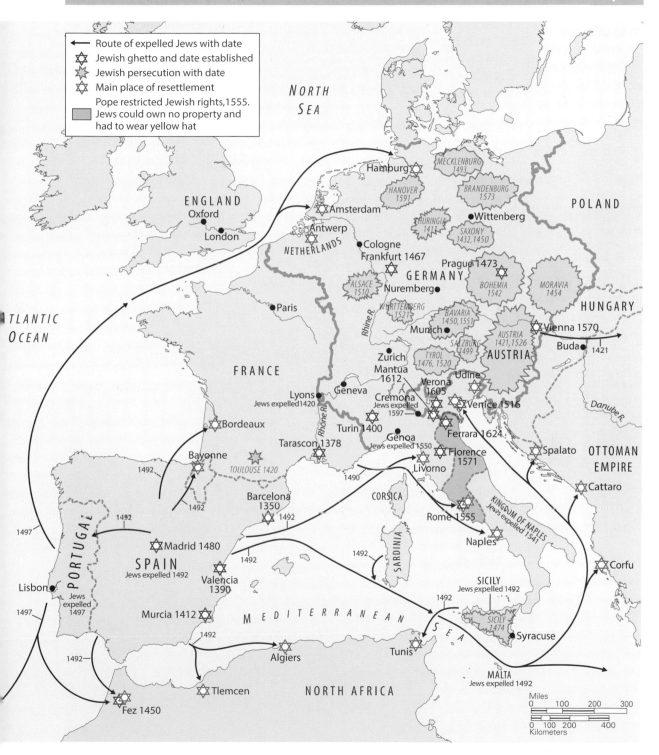

Route of expelled Jews with date
Jewish ghetto and date established
Jewish persecution with date
Main place of resettlement
Pope restricted Jewish rights, 1555.
Jews could own no property and
had to wear yellow hat

NORTH SEA

MECKLENBURG 1493

HANOVER 1591

BRANDENBURG 1573

POLAND

Hamburg

ENGLAND
Oxford
London

Amsterdam

Antwerp

NETHERLANDS

Cologne

Frankfurt 1467

THURINGIA 1411

Wittenberg

SAXONY 1432, 1450

GERMANY

Prague 1473

BOHEMIA 1542

MORAVIA 1454

HUNGARY

ALSACE 1510

Nuremberg

Paris

WÜRTTEMBERG 1521

BAVARIA 1450, 1551

Munich

Rhine R.

AUSTRIA 1421, 1526

Vienna 1570

Buda 1421

ATLANTIC OCEAN

FRANCE

Zurich

Geneva

Lyons
Jews expelled 1420

Rhône R.

Mantua 1612

SALZBURG 1499

TYROL 1476, 1520

Cremona
Jews expelled 1597

Udine

Verona 1605

Venice 1516

Danube R.

Bordeaux

Tarascon 1378

Turin 1400

Genoa
Jews expelled 1550

Ferrara 1624

Spalato

OTTOMAN EMPIRE

Bayonne

1492

TOULOUSE 1420

1492

Barcelona 1350

1492

CORSICA

1490

Florence 1571

Livorno

KINGDOM OF NAPLES
Jews expelled 1541

Cattaro

1497

PORTUGAL

1492

Madrid 1480

SPAIN
Jews expelled 1492

Valencia 1390

1492

1492

SARDINIA

1492

Rome 1555

Naples

Corfu

Lisbon
Jews expelled 1497

1497

Murcia 1412

1492

MEDITERRANEAN

1492

SICILY
Jews expelled 1492

SICILY 1474

Syracuse

1492

Algiers

SEA

Tunis

MALTA
Jews expelled 1492

1492

Tlemcen

NORTH AFRICA

Fez 1450

Miles
0   100   200   300

0   100 200   400
Kilometers

Philipp Melanchthon

After Luther's death Philipp Melanchthon (1497–1560), born at Bretten, near Karlsruhe, took over theological leadership of the movement that Luther had instigated. Something of a prodigy – the University of Heidelberg turned him down for a master's degree because he was only fifteen – Melanchthon began to publish at the age of seventeen and in 1518 was appointed Professor of Greek at the new University of Wittenberg. There he met Luther in a decisive encounter that transformed him from a humanist to a theologian and reformer. With his gift for logical consistency and wide knowledge of history, in some ways Melanchthon influenced Protestantism more strongly than Luther, whose work he consolidated and systematized.

Melanchthon publicly supported Luther at the Leipzig Disputation in 1519, and when Luther was away from Wittenberg represented and defended him. In 1521, he wrote his *Commonplaces* (*Loci communes*), the first book to set out systematically the teachings of the Reformation. He also contributed to Luther's German translation of the Bible. At the Marburg Colloquy of 1529 Melanchthon opposed Zwingli, claiming the service of holy communion was more than a memorial.

Luther himself was little influenced by Humanism; even in his hymns and exegesis he remained a preacher. Melanchthon, by contrast, combined the irenical style of an intellectual debater with the devotion to education of a teacher. He wrote the Augsburg Confession (1530), which remains the chief statement of faith in the Lutheran churches, in part to emphasize the common ground between Catholics and Protestants, and he also participated in important attempts at Christian reunion in 1540 and 1541. Melanchthon often seemed prepared to concede some matters of doctrine to the Roman Catholics for the sake of peace, believing reunion to be essential.

Melanchthon's influence was crucial in what ultimately became the Lutheran Church, although theological struggles with other Lutherans deeply troubled him. In 1548, two years after Luther's death, he accepted an agreement called the Leipzig Interim

Philipp Melanchthon (1497–1560).

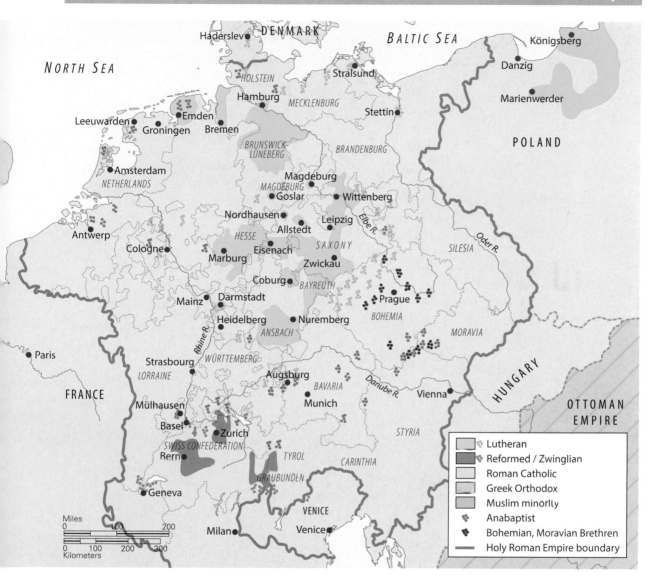

that re-established, among other things, the Latin Mass, the festival of Corpus Christi, and extreme unction. He claimed these were 'things indifferent' (*adiaphora*), but was denounced by Matthias Flacius (1520–75) and the Lutheran theological world divided. Years of doctrinal argument ended only when agreement was reached in the Formula of Concord (1577–80), which reaffirmed the sinner's total spiritual inability and God's unconditional predestination of the elect to faith, but also claimed that an external call to salvation reaches all people and that finally it is possible to fall from grace.

Luther had called upon German princes to carry through church reform if the pope and bishops failed to do so, but by 1529 the territories controlled by princes supporting Luther was still quite limited. Lutheranism had faced several potentially disastrous events in the mid-1520s. The problems with extremists in Wittenberg had led to open conflict and defections from the movement, as had a furious debate between Luther and Erasmus on the freedom of the will. In addition, the Peasants' Revolt lost the Lutherans much of their lower-class support.

Despite these reverses, the movement had expanded after the Edict of Worms (1521). Charles V had left Germany to deal with revolt in Spain and with threats from Francis I of France and Suleiman the Magnificent, and did not return until 1529. These nine years of imperial absence were of immeasurable benefit to the spread and strengthening of the Reformation in Germany.

With Charles not present, the Diet of Speyer in 1526 made a vague ruling on religion: 'Every estate should so live, rule, and believe as he may hope to answer to God and his imperial majesty.' Rulers such as Philipp, Landgrave of Hesse (r. 1518-67), an early and staunch defender of the Protestant cause, used this to justify their action in establishing a Lutheran church in their lands. Yet reformed areas such as Saxony, Hesse, Brunswick-Lüneberg, Ansbach, and other small isolated scattered outposts of Lutheranism were surrounded by Catholic territories.

Marburg Colloquy

In 1529 Philip of Hesse summoned a gathering of reforming theologians to his castle in Marburg for a colloquy, with the aim of achieving an evangelical alliance. Among those attending were Luther himself; Melanchthon; Johannes Bugenhagen (1485–1558), a Wittenberg ally of Luther who later led the reformation in Hamburg; Justus Jonas (1493–1555), who helped reorganize the university at Wittenberg and led the reformation in Halle; Andreas Osiander (1498–1552), an evangelical

preacher in Nuremberg; Johann Agricola (1494–1566), reformer at Frankfurt-am-Main and Eisleben, and later church superintendent in Berlin; Johannes Brenz (1499–1570), reformer of Württemberg and reorganizer of the university in Tübingen; Martin Bucer; Huldrych Zwingli; and Johann Oecolampadius (1482–1531), who led reform in the Swiss cantons of Basel and Bern. The colloquy participants reached agreement on many points, but remained irreconcilably divided over their understanding of the Eucharist.

At the Diet of Speyer (1529) a Catholic majority attempted to prohibit the further spread of Lutheranism and to ensure toleration for Catholics in Lutheran territories. The Lutheran princes 'protested' against this – thereby originating the term 'Protestant'.

Diet of Augsburg

At the ensuing Imperial Diet at Augsburg (1530), attended by Charles V, there were high hopes of re-uniting the opposing parties on the basis of points agreed at Marburg. The Lutherans submitted their beliefs in the form of the Augsburg Confession (or *Augustana*); Strasbourg, Constance, Memmingen, and Lindau presented the Tetrapolitan Confession; and Zwingli sent his *Fidei Ratio*. But the Catholics refused all of these and the Emperor ordered a recess. The Protestant princes realized that the Emperor now intended to make war on Protestantism, so formed in response the Schmalkaldic League.

Holy Roman Empire
Holy Roman Empire boundary
Schmalkadic League of Protestant
rulers and towns, late 1530s

DENMARK

BALTIC SEA

NORTH SEA

POMERANIA

POLAND

Lübeck

Hamburg

Bremen

BRUNSWICK-
LÜNEBERG

c. 1518 Melanchthon joins
Luther's reform activities
1521 Publishes first
Lutheran theological work
Professor at University for 42 years

Berlin

Amsterdam

Oder R.

Wittenberg

ANHALT

Kassel

Leipzig
1519 Attends
Leipzig disputation

SAXONY

Elbe R.

HESSE

Cologne

Schmalkalden
1537 Draws up
Schmalkald Articles

SAXONY

SAXONY

Frankfurt

Mainz

Prague

LUXEMBOURG

PALATINATE

1529 At 2nd Diet of Speyer
Term 'Protestant' first used

Heidelberg

Nuremberg

Speyer

Regensburg

Rhine R.

WÜRTTEMBERG

FRANCE

Strasbourg

Stuttgart

Danube R.

Tübingen

BAVARIA

AUSTRIA

Vienna

Miles
0   50   100   150

Augsburg
1530 Leading Reformer at Diet
Prepares Augsburg Confession

Memmingen

0   50   100   200
Kilometers

Lutheranism Consolidates

When the papal legate formed a league of German princes loyal to Rome, Philip of Hesse created in 1531 a defensive alliance of princes and cities friendly to reform and known as the Schmalkaldic League, consisting of Brandenburg, Mecklenburg, Mansfeld, Magdeburg, Nuremberg, Augsburg, Ulm, and Strasbourg. Prince Albert of Hohenzollern, Grand Master of the Teutonic Knights, also crossed over to the Lutherans, bringing East Prussia with him.

This Protestant alliance was not tested immediately because a threatened Turkish invasion produced a truce between the Emperor and the Schmalkaldic League in 1532. Charles V was then away from Germany until 1541, fighting a series of wars with Francis I of France. Meanwhile Philip of Hesse intervened in Württemberg to restore the Protestant Duke Ulrich to his throne, thereby compelling Charles V's brother to relinquish his claim to the duchy.

By means of conferences at Hagenau, Worms, and Regensburg between 1540 and 1541, designed to find some form of compromise between Catholics and Protestants, Charles V tried to persuade the papacy to participate in efforts at church reconciliation. But Rome was suspicious of these, as were hard-line Lutherans.

In 1546 Charles V returned to Germany determined finally to suppress Protestantism. Things now looked propitious for him. Luther had died the same year, and Philip of Hesse had lost public esteem as a result of his bigamous marriage.

The cathedral and Danube river, Regensburg, Bavaria, Germany.

Schmalkaldic War

The Schmalkaldic War broke out in 1547. The Emperor defeated the Protestant forces and imprisoned their leaders Philip of Hesse and his brother-in-law, John of Saxony. But the Protestant Maurice of Saxony – who initially supported the Emperor – changed sides and fought back successfully. By the Treaty of Passau (1552) Protestantism was legally recognized, a settlement confirmed in the 'Interim' of 1555.

This attempt to settle the religious issues without a church council resulted in a compromise acceptable neither to the Protestants nor the Catholics; only the presence of Spanish troops in northern Europe kept it in force. The so-called War of Liberation followed in which an alliance between Maurice, Elector of Saxony and Henry II of France led to the defeat of Charles V and his flight across the Alps. The ensuing Peace of Augsburg (1555) showed significant Protestant gains compared with 1529.

Huldrych Zwingli

The Swiss Reformer Huldrych Zwingli (1484–1531) was born in Wildhaus, north-east Switzerland. Educated in Basel, Berne, and Vienna, between 1506 and 1516 he was vicar at Glarus, where he learned Greek and possibly Hebrew, and studied the Church Fathers. He acted as chaplain to Swiss mercenary forces at the battle of Novara (1513) and at Marignano (1515), an experience that led him to oppose the use of mercenary soldiers.

In 1515 Zwingli met Erasmus and was deeply influenced by his Humanist teaching. After his forced transfer to Einsiedeln, Zwingli began to develop evangelical beliefs as he reflected on abuses in the church. In 1518 he was made peoples' priest at Zurich's Grossmünster (cathedral), where he lectured on the New Testament and began to reform the city, working closely with the council. Luther's writings and example helped convert Zwingli from criticism of corruption in the church to a passionate reformer who wanted to win Zurich to the evangelical cause. When Zwingli won a disputation at Bern in 1528, Basel, Gall, Schaffhausen, and Constance all joined the reform movement.

Zwingli was a close friend and confidant of Philip of Hesse, the most influential Protestant prince in Germany. Together they conceived a Protestant federation extending from Switzerland to Denmark, defending Reform against the pope, the emperor, Catholic princes, and the Ottoman Turks. This vision died at the Marburg Colloquy (1529), for Luther would not agree to an

Grossmünster, Zurich.

Huldrych Zwingli (1484–1531).

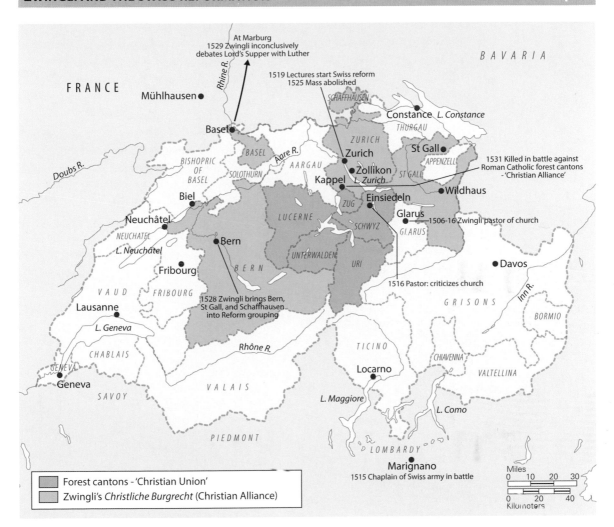

At Marburg
1529 Zwingli inconclusively
debates Lord's Supper with Luther

1519 Lectures start Swiss reform
1525 Mass abolished

BAVARIA

Rhine R.

FRANCE

Mühlhausen●

SCHAFFHAUSEN

Constance *L. Constance*

THURGAU

Basel●

BASEL

Aare R.

BISHOPRIC OF BASEL

AARGAU

ZURICH

Zurich

St Gall

APPENZELL

1531 Killed in battle against
Roman Catholic forest cantons
- 'Christian Alliance'

SOLOTHURN

Zollikon

ST GALL

Kappel *L. Zurich*

Biel

ZUG

Einsiedeln

●Wildhaus

Neuchâtel

LUCERNE

Glarus

1506-16 Zwingli pastor of church

NEUCHÂTEL

L. Neuchâtel

●Bern

SCHWYZ

GLARUS

Fribourg

BERN

UNTERWALDEN

URI

1516 Pastor: criticizes church

●Davos

Inn R.

FRIBOURG

VAUD

1528 Zwingli brings Bern,
St Gall, and Schaffhausen
into Reform grouping

GRISONS

BORMIO

Lausanne

Rhône R.

TICINO

CHIAVENNA

L. Geneva

CHABLAIS

VALAIS

Locarno

VALTELLINA

L. Como

GENEVA

Geneva

SAVOY

L. Maggiore

PIEDMONT

LOMBARDY

Marignano
1515 Chaplain of Swiss army in battle

Miles
0 10 20 30

0   20   40
Kilometers

Forest cantons - 'Christian Union'
Zwingli's *Christliche Burgrecht* (Christian Alliance)

alliance with the Swiss and with Protestant Strasbourg, both of whom denied the real presence in terms of Christ's corporal presence in the elements of the Lord's Supper.

Because of these differences over the Eucharist, the Swiss reform movement forfeited the support of the German princes.

Zwingli now turned to force to establish evangelical preaching in the mountain cantons. The Second Kappel War broke out in 1531 when a blockade led to five Catholic forest cantons sending an army against Zurich. Zwingli was killed at the Battle of Kappel (1531).

HULDRYCH ZWINGLI   71

Martin Bucer (or Butzer, 1491–1551) was born at Sélestat, Alsace, thirty miles south of Strasbourg. He joined the Dominican order as a novice aged fifteen, and later became interested in Humanism and met Luther. In 1521 he was released from the Dominicans, began to preach reform, and in 1522 married a former nun, Elisabeth Silbereisen (c. 1495–1541). The following year he had to take refuge in the tolerant city of Strasbourg, where he led the reform and in 1540 became superintendent of the churches.

At Strasbourg he held discussions and public debates with radical reformers and started house-meetings to improve Christian living among preachers and laypeople. In a vitriolic age, Bucer was notable for his compassion, dedicating himself to church unity. He became one of the Reformers' chief statesmen, attending most of their important conferences and colloquies. In an effort to unite the German and Swiss Reformed churches, Bucer strove to mediate between Zwingli and Luther. He also took part in ultimately unsuccessful conferences with Roman Catholics at Hagenau, Worms, and Ratisbon.

Hesse

Bucer worked as advisor to the Landgrave Philip I in the reformation of Hesse. After Bucer held a series of sympathetic debates, hundreds of Anabaptists in Hesse rejoined the official Protestant church in 1538, a conversion unique in the sixteenth century, when rulers usually dealt with Anabaptists by expulsion, persecution, or execution. Bucer also assisted the Archbishop-Elector Hermann von Wied (1477–1552) in his vain attempt to reform the church in Cologne. Bucer developed an evangelical rite of confirmation, which spread from Strasbourg to Swiss and German Protestants, and later to Anglicanism.

Cambridge

After Bucer resisted the Emperor's religious settlement, the Augsburg Interim, he was forced to leave Strasbourg in 1549, fleeing to Cambridge, England. Around this time

Martin Bucer (1491–1551).

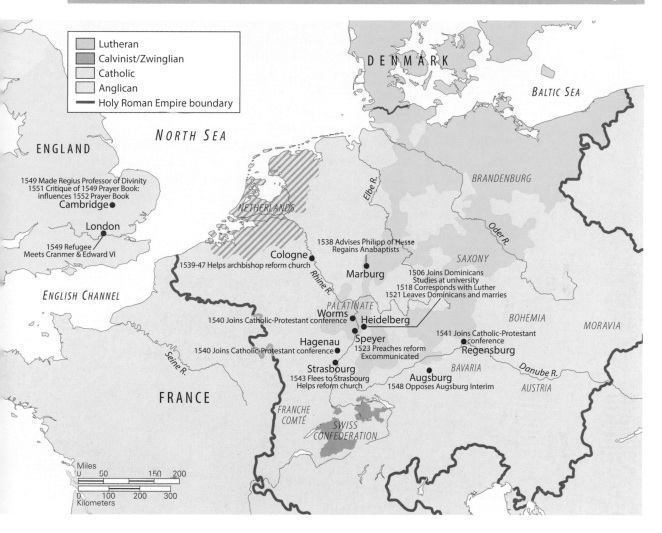

Legend:
- Lutheran
- Calvinist/Zwinglian
- Catholic
- Anglican
- Holy Roman Empire boundary

DENMARK

BALTIC SEA

NORTH SEA

ENGLAND

BRANDENBURG

1549 Made Regius Professor of Divinity
1551 Critique of 1549 Prayer Book:
influences 1552 Prayer Book
Cambridge ●

NETHERLANDS

Elbe R.

Oder R.

SAXONY

London

1549 Refugee
Meets Cranmer & Edward VI

Cologne ●
1539-47 Helps archbishop reform church

Rhine R.

1538 Advises Philipp of Hesse
Regains Anabaptists

Marburg ●

1506 Joins Dominicans
Studies at university
1518 Corresponds with Luther
1521 Leaves Dominicans and marries

ENGLISH CHANNEL

PALATINATE

Worms ●
1540 Joins Catholic-Protestant conference

Heidelberg ●

BOHEMIA

MORAVIA

1541 Joins Catholic-Protestant
● conference

Hagenau ●
1540 Joins Catholic-Protestant conference

Seine R.

Speyer
1523 Preaches reform
Excommunicated

Regensburg ●

FRANCE

Strasbourg ●
1543 Flees to Strasbourg
Helps reform church

BAVARIA

Augsburg ●
1548 Opposes Augsburg Interim

Danube R.

AUSTRIA

FRANCHE
COMTÉ

SWISS
CONFEDERATION

Miles
0   50   150   200

0   100   200   300
Kilometers

Archbishop Cranmer welcomed many prominent overseas Reformers displaced by Catholic victories in central Europe, particularly non-Lutherans such as Peter Martyr Vermigli (1499–1562), Jan Łaski (John a Lasco 1499–1560), and Martin Bucer, with whom he had been quietly corresponding for several years. With the advice and support of Vermigli and Bucer, Cranmer produced his second Prayer Book in 1552, far more radical than the stop-gap version of 1549. Martin Bucer died in Cambridge in 1551, but his body was exhumed and burned during the Catholic reaction under Mary Tudor.

John Calvin

The Genevan Reformer Jean (John) Calvin (1509–64) was an important shaper of the Reformed tradition in Protestantism, a position already defined by such Reformers as Zwingli, Bullinger, Bucer, Oecolampadius, and Vermigli. Born at Noyon, Picardy, northern France, in contrast to Luther, Calvin was a quiet, sensitive man with an immovable will. Calvin studied Latin and philosophy in Paris, followed by civil law at the universities of Orléans and Bourges, where he also learned Greek. He soon took up the methods of Humanism. In Paris, the young Calvin encountered the teachings of Luther, and around 1533 experienced conversion: 'God subdued and brought my heart to docility.' He broke with Roman Catholicism, fled persecution in Paris in 1533, and found refuge in Angoulême, Noyon, and Orleans. Calvin finally left France and lived as an exile in Basel, where he began to formulate his theology, and in 1536 published the first edition of *Christianae Religionis Institutio* (*The Institution of the Christian Religion*, better known as the *Institutes*), a brief, clear statement of Reformation beliefs.

In 1536 Calvin visited Ferrara briefly and, en route to Strasbourg, was prevailed upon by Guillaume Farel (1489–1565), the Reformer of Geneva, to help consolidate the Reformation there. But Genevans opposed Calvin's efforts, and disputes in the town and a quarrel with the city of Bern resulted in the expulsion of both Calvin and Farel in 1538.

Calvin now fled to Strasbourg, where he was encouraged and influenced by Martin Bucer. The years in this city, where he ministered to the French Protestant refugees and taught theology, were among his happiest. In March 1540 Calvin published his commentary on Paul's Letter to the Romans, followed by other commentaries and a new, enlarged version of the *Institutes*. Calvin continued to rewrite and expand the *Institutes*, which became a classic statement of Reformation theology; by the final 1559 edition, the original six chapters had become eighty. Calvin was a great systematizer, taking up and reapplying the ideas of the first generation of Reformers.

Return to Geneva

In September 1541 Calvin was invited back to Geneva, where he now tried to bring the citizens under the moral discipline of the

John Calvin (1509–64).

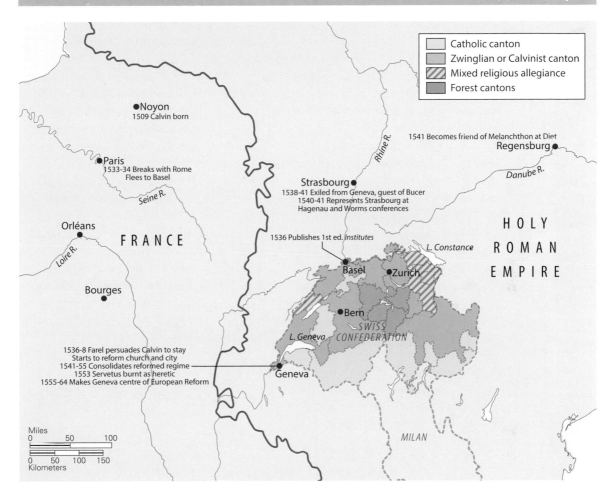

Catholic canton
Zwinglian or Calvinist canton
Mixed religious allegiance
Forest cantons

●Noyon
1509 Calvin born

1541 Becomes friend of Melanchthon at Diet
Regensburg●

Rhine R.

●Paris
1533-34 Breaks with Rome
Flees to Basel

Danube R.

Seine R.

Strasbourg●
1538-41 Exiled from Geneva, guest of Bucer
1540-41 Represents Strasbourg at
Hagenau and Worms conferences

Orléans
●

F R A N C E

1536 Publishes 1st ed. *Institutes*

L. Constance

H O L Y

R O M A N

Basel
●Zurich

E M P I R E

Bourges
●

●Bern

SWISS
CONFEDERATION

L. Geneva

1536-8 Farel persuades Calvin to stay
Starts to reform church and city
1541-55 Consolidates reformed regime
1553 Servetus burnt as heretic
1555-64 Makes Geneva centre of European Reform

Geneva

MILAN

Miles
0   50   100

0   50   100   150
Kilometers

church, aiming to create a 'mature' church by preaching daily to the people. Many resented his strictures, especially as they were imposed by a foreigner.

Calvin also devoted energy to settling differences within Protestantism. The *Consensus Tigurinus* on the Lord's Supper (1549) resulted in the German- and French-speaking churches of Switzerland moving closer together. In 1553 the Spaniard Michael Servetus (1509/11–53), a notorious critic of Calvin and of the doctrine of the Trinity, was arrested and burnt in Geneva. Already

on the run from the Inquisition, Servetus was regarded by all as a heretic; Protestant reformers felt they could not afford to be seen as soft on heresy.

Calvin wanted to build a visible 'City of God' in Europe – with Geneva as a starting-point. He founded the Geneva Academy, to which students of theology came from all parts of western and central Europe, and particularly France. Calvin remained in Geneva the rest of his life, training missionaries to export reform, especially back to France.

By 1513 Switzerland consisted of thirteen cantons – six rural and seven urban – along with a number of allied states. During the fifteenth century the Swiss had won military victories against Burgundy, Milan, and finally in 1499 the Emperor, and were *de facto* independent. In politics and religion each canton had a high degree of autonomy.

Reformation came to Zurich at the same time as Germany, but independently. Its theology was similar to Luther's, except in the understanding of the Eucharist. By 1528 Bern, Basel (led by Johann Oecolampadius), St Gall, and Schaffhausen had also embraced Reform; shortly after this Guillaume Farel (1489–1565) introduced Reform in Neuchâtel and Geneva.

In 1524 the four traditionally conservative mountain cantons formed a Christian Union to resist Reform; in response the Zwinglians of Zurich and Constance formed their own Christian Alliance (1527), joined later by others.

After Zwingli's untimely death at the Battle of Kappel (1531), the leadership in Zurich passed to Heinrich Bullinger (1504–75), who produced the *Consensus Tigurinus* (1549), a lengthy essay on the Lord's Supper co-authored with John Calvin, and the *Second Helvetic Confession* (1566), which brought together the German-speaking and French-speaking Reformation parties and was adopted by non-Lutheran churches in Switzerland, Scotland, France, Poland, and Hungary. Bullinger's importance in the Reformation has been widely underestimated: in England he was to become more influential than Calvin.

THE REFORMATION IN SWITZERLAND — map 26

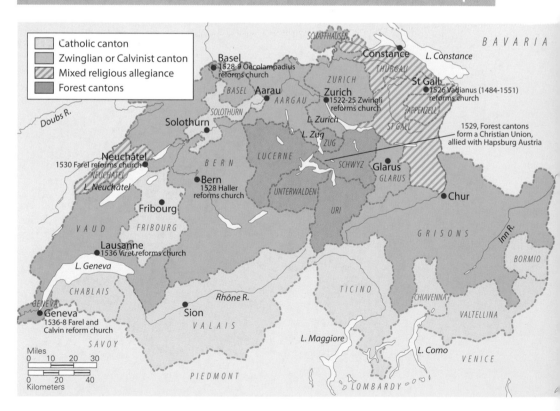

John Calvin set about establishing Geneva as a model Reformed city, which it duly became as a result of his activities and the Academy that he established in 1559 to train reformers for Western Europe, which became the University of Geneva. Geneva also became the print capital of Protestant Europe, with more than thirty presses publishing literature in a number of languages. Calvin's systematized Protestantism, set out in his *Institutes*, quickly became the vehicle of Reformed Protestantism. John Knox, the Scots Protestant leader, called Geneva 'the most perfect school of Christ'.

By 1555 Calvinism was spreading, but had not gained official acceptance apart from in Geneva and the tiny kingdom of Navarre, on the French side of the Pyrenees. Calvinism took early root in many places where Waldensian churches had previously been active.

The most promising area for the growth of Calvinism was France, Calvin's homeland. Many French Protestants came to Geneva to train before carrying Calvin's theology home. In 1559 the Geneva Academy had 162 students; by 1564 more than 1500, mostly foreign. The first Huguenot (Reformed) ministers arrived in France in 1553; by the time of Calvin's death it is estimated some two million French people professed the Reformed faith.

Calvinism also spread early to the Netherlands. Reform ministers first arrived in the 1550s and were supported by Protestant Huguenot preachers fleeing France. They made slow progress at first because they were fiercely opposed by the authorities. Calvinism was initially strongest in Antwerp, Ghent, and areas near Germany, from which it gradually spread northwards.

Calvinism was not even recognized as an option by the German princes in the Peace of Augsburg (1555), and was generally regarded with suspicion by the ruling elite. It first entered Germany via the Netherlands in the 1560s, developing into a popular movement

The Reformation Wall, Geneva: (left to right) Guillaume Farel, Jean Calvin, Theodore Beza, John Knox.

in nearby North-West Rhineland and Westphalia. Some Lutherans were influenced by Calvin, notably Philipp Melanchthon; after Luther's death a number of Melanchthon's followers joined the Reformed Church.

In 1562, the Elector Palatine, Frederick III (r. 1559–76) made Calvinism the official religion in his domain, and under his tutelage the Reformed Heidelberg Catechism (1563) was drawn up. However most of Germany remained Lutheran. Early in the seventeenth century John Sigismund, Elector of Brandenburg (r. 1608–19), converted to Calvinism and after a bitter internal struggle his state permitted both Lutheranism and Calvinism.

By the mid-sixteenth century there was a considerable Protestant movement in Hungary, mainly in the east, where it enjoyed the protection of the princes of Transylvania. Reform came under Calvinist influence and the church became Presbyterian, governed by a pyramid of elected representative courts, or presbyteries.

Calvinism first reached Poland in 1550, when the nobles opportunistically bribed the civilian population with some religious rights in order to increase their own power. The Lithuanian noble Mikołaj 'The Black' Radziwiłł (1515–65) and Polish reformer Jan Łaski (John a Lasco, 1499–1560) helped the spread of Calvinism.

The Reformation spread to Scotland largely due to the activities of John Knox (1513–72), who served as a galley slave before arriving in Calvin's Geneva. Knox exported Calvinist principles from Geneva to Scotland, where he became its most notable spokesman.

When Elizabeth I succeeded to the English throne, her cautious, moderate religious reform disappointed a minority who reacted with a more rigorous form of Calvinism that became known disparagingly as 'Puritanism'.

Calvinist/Reformed
Huguenot centres
Spread of Calvinism
Holy Roman Empire boundary

NORWAY

SWEDEN

NORTH SEA

BALTIC SEA

DENMARK

Copenhagen

PRUSSIA

LITHUANIA

Hamburg

GERMANY

Wittenberg

Vistula R.

Warsaw

Amsterdam

POLAND

NETHERLANDS

Cologne

Leipzig

Elbe R.

Marburg

Oder R.

Brussels

Prague

BOHEMIA

Worms

Speyer

Rhine R.

Danube R.

Paris

Munich

AUSTRIA

TRANSYLVANIA

eans

Dijon

Basel

Buda   Pest

Geneva

SWISS
CONFEDERATION

Zurich

Lyons

SAVOY

Trent

HUNGARY

MILAN

VENICE

Milan

Venice

Avignon

Genoa

GENOA

ouse

Marseilles

PAPAL
STATES

ADRIATIC
SEA

Danube R.

MEDITERRANEAN SEA

Miles
0   100   200   300

0   100   200   400
Kilometers

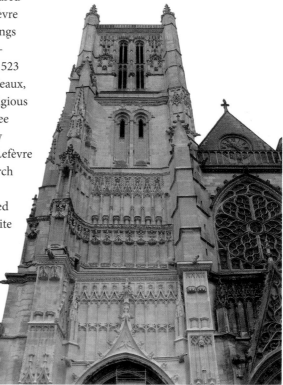

Reform in France

For most of the fourteenth century French kings dominated the papacy and Paris theologians could claim intellectual leadership of the Western church. With the reduction of English power in France, French nationalism surged. From this time, the French king was known as *Rex Christianissimus* ('most Christian king'). Under the able leadership of Louis XI (r. 1461–83), France broke the dominant power of Burgundy.

Inheriting a strong, centralized monarchy, Francis I (r. 1515–47) concluded a treaty of perpetual peace with Switzerland, and signed a concordat with the papacy that brought the French church under his control. In return for guaranteed annates, the pope granted the king the appointment of bishops and abbots. Francis also reached a settlement with Henry VIII of England that freed him to wage war on the Emperor Charles V. This military threat distracted the Emperor, thus helping the spread of Protestantism.

French humanists

The road to reform in France was prepared by two learned humanists: Jacques Lefèvre d'Étaples (c. 1455–1536) – whose writings anticipated much of Luther's teaching – and Guillaume Budé (1467–1540). In 1523 Lefèvre was invited by the Bishop of Meaux, Guillaume Briçonnet, to encourage religious revival in his diocese by distributing free copies of Lefèvre's own vernacular New Testament and by militant preaching. Lefèvre worked for reform within existing church structures and did not repudiate papal authority. This reforming group received support from the king's sister, Marguerite d'Angoulême, herself a writer influenced by humanist thinking.

In February 1525 Francis I was captured by Charles V. His mother Louise became regent and her hostility to reform led Lefèvre and others flee into exile. A year later

Francis was released and Lefèvre returned – but the reform experiment at Meaux was never restarted.

Affair of the *placards*

A crisis of reform in France came on 18 October 1534, when Parisians awoke to find '*placards*' (broadsheets) displayed in public places attacking 'the horrible, great, and insufferable abuses of the papal Mass'. Those responsible were executed, and burnings and persecution followed. The *placard* was the work of a French pastor exiled at Neuchâtel; a network of reform influenced by Swiss

The Cathedral of Saint Etienne, Meaux, France.

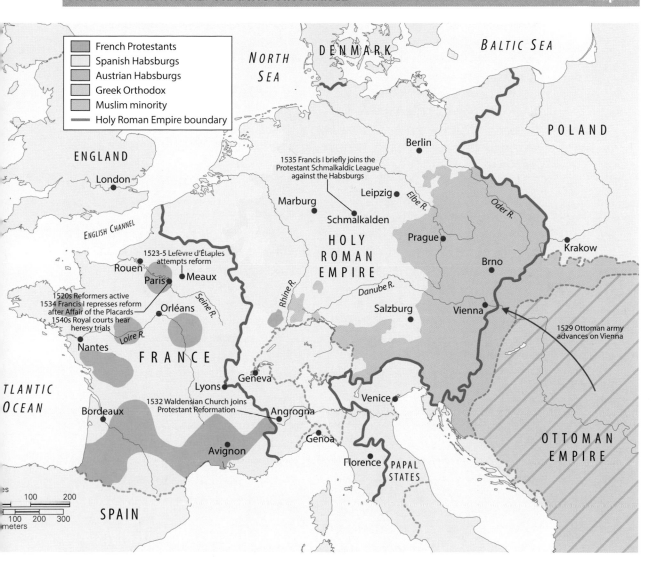

Legend:
- French Protestants
- Spanish Habsburgs
- Austrian Habsburgs
- Greek Orthodox
- Muslim minority
- Holy Roman Empire boundary

1535 Francis I briefly joins the Protestant Schmalkaldic League against the Habsburgs

1523-5 Lefèvre d'Étaples attempts reform

1520s Reformers active
1534 Francis I represses reform after Affair of the Placards
1540s Royal courts hear heresy trials

1532 Waldensian Church joins Protestant Reformation

1529 Ottoman army advances on Vienna

Protestants existed in France. In 1533 John Calvin fled Paris as he was a known associate of Nicolas Cop, Rector of the university and an advocate of Reform.

The king's attitude to Reform now hardened and in 1540 the royal courts took over heresy trials from the more lenient church tribunals. Meanwhile many Reformers continued to work under the cover of conformity, a pattern pioneered by Lefèvre. Many priests and friars preached Reforming sermons – sometimes to large crowds – and held private sessions for prayer or Bible study. They evaded prosecution by minimal conformity, continuing to hear confessions and celebrate Mass. Calvin fiercely opposed such occasional conformity, comparing it to the biblical Jewish leader Nicodemus, who met Christ under cover of darkness.

Scandinavian Reform

Between 1397 and 1523 the Union of Kalmar brought together the Scandinavian nations under a single monarch who ruled the three kingdoms of Denmark, Sweden (including Finland), and Norway (including Iceland, Greenland, and the Faroe Islands). In 1520 Gustav Vasa organized a successful revolt and became king of an independent Sweden, which under his dynasty became the strongest Baltic power.

Two brothers, Olaus and Laurentius Petri (Olof, 1493–1552 and Lars Persson, 1499–1573), both disciples of Luther, inaugurated religious reform in Sweden. Aided by Laurentius Andreae (Lars Andersson, c. 1470–1552), they brought the evangelical theology of Luther to the Swedish church. In 1527 the Reformation was established by law; church lands were secularized and bishops of the old church were incorporated into the new. Reform was completed at the Synod of Uppsala in 1593, when the Lutheran Augsburg Confession was adopted as the sole basis of faith.

Denmark

In 1500, the church owned roughly one-third of the land of Denmark. The new university of Copenhagen, founded in 1478, became an early centre of Reforming protest. In 1524 the exiled King Christian II commissioned a (much criticized) Danish version of the New Testament. Meanwhile Frederick I (r. 1524–33) pressed for church reform, appointing Reforming bishops and preachers. Danes such as Hans Tausen (1494–1561) and Jørgen Sadolin (c. 1490–1559), who had studied under Luther at Wittenberg, started to preach Lutheranism. There was a rapid defection of Catholics and in some places there was no preaching, or services were held only two or three times a year.

When Christian III (r. 1534–59) succeeded to the Danish throne, the transition to Protestantism was completed. At the Diet of Copenhagen (1536) he stripped the bishops of their property, transferring the church's wealth to the state. He then turned for help to Luther, who in 1537 sent Johannes Bugenhagen (1485–1558) to crown the king and appoint seven church superintendents. At the synods that followed, church ordinances were published and the Reformation recognized in Danish law. The University of Copenhagen was enlarged and revitalized, a new Protestant liturgy drawn up, a new translation of the Bible completed, and a modified version of the Augsburg Confession eventually adopted.

Norway

In 1537 Christian attempted to extend the Reformation to Norway – which remained under Danish rule – though with little popular support. Most bishops fled, and as the older clergy died they were replaced with Reforming ministers. In 1571 Jorgen Eriksson, the 'Norwegian Luther', was appointed Bishop of Stavanger; but not till three years after he died, in 1604, was a Lutheran church order formally established.

Iceland

Christian III also expelled the Roman Catholic bishops in Iceland and confiscated their property. His initial attempt to impose the new Danish ecclesiastical system there provoked a revolt but he eventually succeeded in establishing Reform. Through an Icelandic hymnal (1589) and first complete Icelandic Bible translation (1584), both created by Bishop Gudbrandur Thorlaksson (1541–1627), the Old Norse tongue was saved and the Reformation became popular.

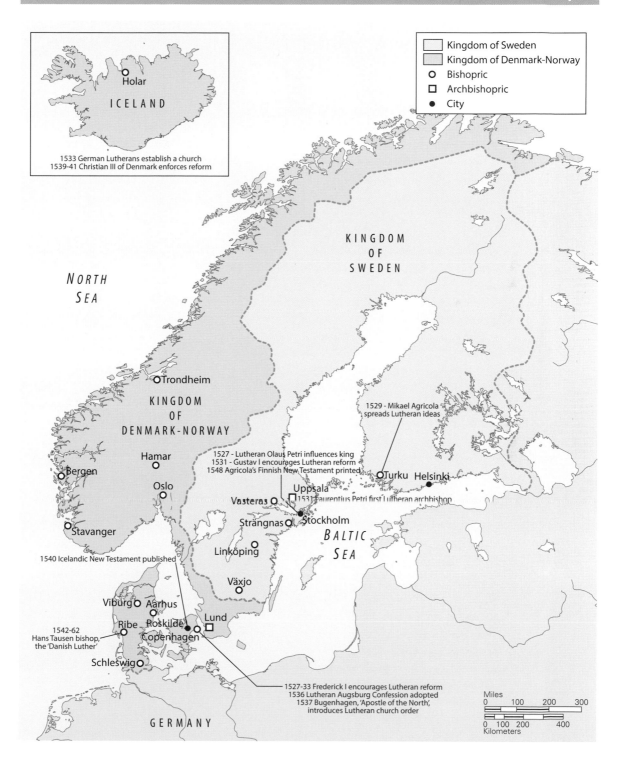

Kingdom of Sweden
Kingdom of Denmark-Norway
○ Bishopric
□ Archbishopric
● City

Holar
ICELAND
1533 German Lutherans establish a church
1539-41 Christian III of Denmark enforces reform

KINGDOM
OF
SWEDEN

NORTH
SEA

Trondheim

KINGDOM
OF
DENMARK-NORWAY

1529 - Mikael Agricola
spreads Lutheran ideas

Hamar

Bergen

Oslo

1527 - Lutheran Olaus Petri influences king
1531 - Gustav I encourages Lutheran reform
1548 Agricola's Finnish New Testament printed

Turku Helsinki

Uppsala
1531 Laurentius Petri first Lutheran archbishop

Vasteras

Strängnas   Stockholm

Stavanger

BALTIC
SEA

1540 Icelandic New Testament published

Linköping

Växjo

Viburg   Aarhus

Ribe   Roskilde   Lund

1542-62
Hans Tausen bishop,
the 'Danish Luther'

Copenhagen

Schleswig

1527-33 Frederick I encourages Lutheran reform
1536 Lutheran Augsburg Confession adopted
1537 Bugenhagen, 'Apostle of the North',
introduces Lutheran church order

Miles
0   100   200   300

0 100 200   400
Kilometers

GERMANY

Dissolution

The greatest material change effected by Henry VIII's Reformation was the destruction of England's religious houses. In 1532 about 800 corporate religious foundations were standing England and Wales; by 1540 all had gone. Monasteries had represented half the church's assets and were deeply rooted in local communities. The revolution in landownership resulting from their dissolution was 'second only to that which followed the Norman Conquest' (Youings).

Henry was convinced the church had become wealthy at the crown's expense. In 1536, legislation was passed listing smaller, less viable, monasteries for closure and around half were dissolved. Monks from these houses were either given pensions or moved to larger houses. Stories of roaming hordes of homeless religious are a myth as are tales of hundreds of abbey servants thrown out of work: they continued as farm labourers when church estates passed to the crown. There was however considerable looting and the nobility and gentry competed to lease or buy monastic property.

The Pilgrimage of Grace transformed Henry VIII's attitude towards monasticism; after it he became completely hostile. From late 1537 the government began to pressurize religious houses to surrender – both those reprieved earlier and the larger abbeys. Waltham Abbey, Essex, the last to surrender, went down in April 1540. With no houses left to move to, the religious were pensioned off. The four orders of friars were also suppressed, along with the Order of St John of Jerusalem. Just six abbeys were salvaged to be subsequently refounded as cathedrals: Westminster Abbey, Gloucester, Peterborough, Oxford, Bristol, and Chester.

map 30

THE DISSOLUTION OF THE ENGLISH MONASTERIES

······ Boundaries of bishoprics pre-1540

☐ Greater monasteries dissolved 1538-40 (not comprehensive). Numbers following name = number of monastic houses in town

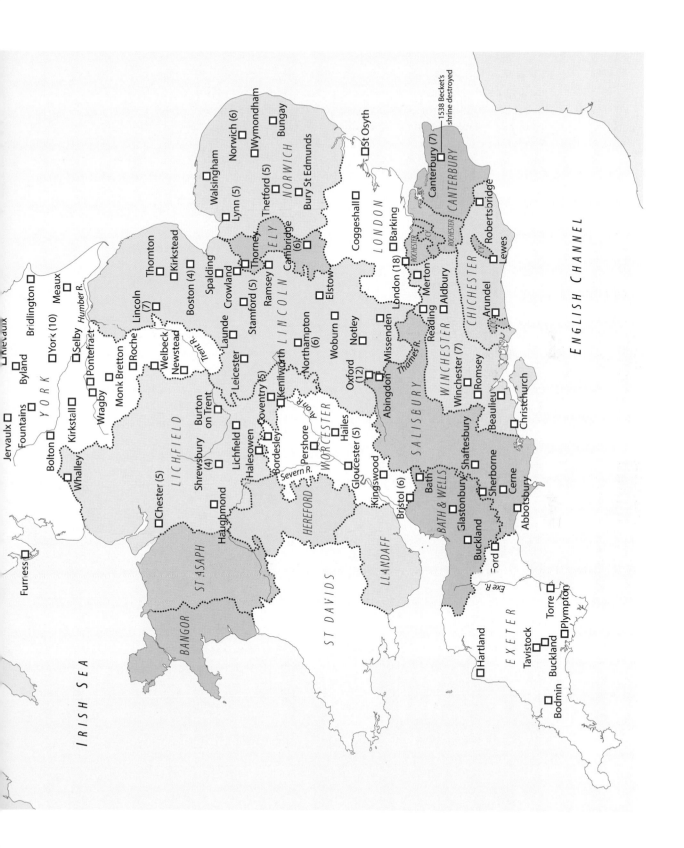

IRISH SEA

ENGLISH CHANNEL

1538 Becket's shrine destroyed

Jervaulx
Furress
Fountains
Byland
Bridlington
York (10)
Meaux
Humber R.
Selby
Bolton
Kirkstall
Whalley
Pontefract
Monk Bretton
Roche
Wragby
Welbeck
Newstead
Trent R.
Lincoln (7)
Boston (4)
Spalding
Crowland
Laude
Leicester
Thornton
Kirkstead

YORK

LICHFIELD

Chester (5)
Shrewsbury (4)
Lichfield
Halesowen
Burton on Trent
Bordesley
Coventry (5)
Kenilworth
Pershore
Avon R.
Hailes
Kingswood
Gloucester (5)
Bristol (6)

Haughmond

HEREFORD

WORCESTER

Severn R.

BANGOR

ST ASAPH

ST DAVIDS

LLANDAFF

Walsingham
Lynn (5)
Norwich (6)
Wymondham
Bungay
Thetford (5)
Bury St Edmunds

NORWICH

ELY

Thorney
Ramsey
Cambridge (6)
Stamford (5)
Northampton (6)
Woburn
Elstow
Notley

LINCOLN

Coggeshall
St Osyth
Barking

LONDON

London (18)
Merton
Reading
Aldbury
Missenden
Oxford (12)
Abingdon
Thames R.
Reading

ROCHESTER

Canterbury (7)

CANTERBURY

CHICHESTER

Robertsbridge
Lewes
Arundel

Romsey
Beaulieu
Christchurch

WINCHESTER

Winchester (7)

SALISBURY

Bath
Glastonbury
Shaftesbury
Sherborne
Cerne
Abbotsbury
Buckland
Ford

BATH & WELLS

Exe R.

EXETER

Hartland
Tavistock
Buckland
Torre
Plympton
Bodmin

The Pilgrimage of Grace was the largest and most menacing of a succession of Tudor rebellions, although those taking part regarded it as protest not rebellion. During the summer of 1536 a series of radical alterations in religion occurred in England: clergy were required to know and do new things, treasures in parish churches appeared to be under threat, and smaller monasteries were being dissolved.

The coincidental presence in Lincolnshire of three sets of commissioners – one overseeing the dissolution of lesser monasteries, another a visitation to the clergy, and a third gathering gentry to deal with taxation – encouraged a riot in the town of Louth to grow rapidly into insurrection in much of the county and occupation of the city of Lincoln. Soon about 20,000 men were up in arms, although the movement quickly fizzled out.

Yorkshire

As things quietened in Lincolnshire, the movement crossed into Yorkshire, prompted by similar fears about the supposed threat to traditional religion. The lawyer Robert Aske (1500–37) invented the name 'Pilgrimage of Grace', declaring himself 'chief captain',

Ruins of Rievaulx Abbey, Yorkshire.

and defining it as a movement for the defence of the church and the removal of the king's 'heretical' councillors, especially the Chancellor Thomas Cromwell and Archbishop Thomas Cranmer. The protesters marched with a badge displaying the five wounds of Christ. The Lincolnshire Rising and the Pilgrimage of Grace amounted to a huge northern demonstration opposing Henry's policies.

Despite significant involvement of the gentry and some nobles, the main support came from the lower clergy, yeomen, and craftsmen – all commoners. As the disturbances spread north-westwards, resentment against landlords and their renting and leasing policies also grew. Soon the pilgrims had nine regional armies – perhaps 50,000 armed men – and held the whole of England north of the River Trent. The Duke of Norfolk managed to negotiate a truce, the Pilgrims began to disperse, and the gentry deposed Aske, regained control, and allowed individuals to make terms with the government.

Revenge

But Henry VIII was not interested in conciliation. He strung out discussions until he was in a position to launch his revenge. Abortive secondary episodes in 1537, led by the maverick Sir Francis Bigod, gave the king the excuse he needed to take reprisals. While the rank and file melted back into obscurity, Henry proceeded to execute the leaders of the Pilgrimage. Henry VIII was now able to continue as head of the church without let or hindrance.

Monasteries involved in Pilgrimage of Grace
Monasteries whose abbot was executed by Henry VIII
Area affected by Pilgrimage of Grace 1536-7
Route of Lincolnshire rebels
Routes of Yorkshire rebels
Route of Kirkby Stephen & Cumberland rebels
Route of Westmorland rebels
Boundaries of bishoprics pre-1540

SCOTLAND

Lanercost
Carlisle
Newcastle
Cockermouth
Penrith
Durham
Bishop Auckland
Kirkby Stephen
Barnard Castle
Whitby
Kendal
Richmond
Jervaulx
Scarborough
Cartmel
Sedbergh
Masham
Bridlington
Ripon
Lancaster
Fountains
York
Sawley
Skipton
Nunburnholme
Whalley
Pontefract
Humber R.
Hull
Manchester
Doncaster
Caister
Sheffield
Louth
Lincoln
Barlings
Legbourne
Chester
Bardney
Horncastle
Kirkstead
Derby
Trent R.
Lenton

NORTH SEA

ENGLAND

WALES
Severn R.
Avon R.
Woburn
Oxford
Colchester
Bristol
London
Thames R.
Glastonbury
Canterbury

Miles
0 10 20 30 40 50
0 10 20 30 40 50
Kilometers

1525-6: William Tyndale publishes English New Testament
1531: Henry VIII 'Supreme Head of Church of England'
1534: Act of Supremacy: Church of England breaks with Rome
1539: Henry VIII issues Catholic 'Six Articles'; repealed 1547
1525
1530
1535
1540
1533: Pope excommunicates Henry VIII
1536: Dissolution of monasteries begins

The struggle between the old and the new lasted longer in England than elsewhere in Europe. As early as the thirteenth century an anti-papal, anti-clerical movement had developed, when Wyclif had fathered an evangelical protest movement. Early in the sixteenth century Luther's writings and English Bibles were smuggled into England. At first the Reform movement was Lutheran, but Reform soon became entangled with politics. In 1534 King Henry VIII proclaimed himself the Head of the Church of England, though his quarrel with the pope was not on religious grounds, but because the pope would not sanction Henry's desired divorce of Catherine of Aragon. Henry himself remained a Catholic: the pope entitled him 'Defender of the Faith' for a book he wrote opposing Luther in 1521, and in 1539 Henry issued the Six Articles, probably aiming to limit the progress of Reform. Henry now removed the authority of the pope and ended monasticism in England, while among some of his people a religious movement towards Reform was also occurring. The University of Cambridge was one centre of Reformation thinking and the appearance of Tyndale's English New Testament (1525) also aided the cause of Reform.

Under Edward VI (r. 1547–53) the Reformation moved sharply forwards, led by the Archbishop of Canterbury, Thomas Cranmer, supported by Bishops Nicholas Ridley (c. 1500–55) and Hugh Latimer (c. 1487–1555). Several European Calvinist Reformers also contributed, notably Martin Bucer from Strasbourg, Peter Martyr Vermigli from Italy, who became professors at Oxford and Cambridge, and John a Lasco from Poland.

Mary Tudor

Following Edward's premature death, Henry's daughter Mary Tudor (r. 1553–58) attempted to restore Roman Catholicism and the authority of the pope to England, with the help of Cardinal Reginald Pole (1500–58). But her inability to understand Protestantism actually did much to strengthen the movement by creating many martyrs. About 290 bishops and scholars – including Cranmer, Latimer, and Ridley – and other men and women were burnt at the stake, many others fleeing to Europe.

Elizabeth I

Mary's sister Elizabeth restored and permanently established Protestantism in England during her long reign (r. 1558–1603). She faced considerable difficulties, including the threat of civil war, the theological and political opposition of the Catholic powers, the hostility of France and Spain, and doubts about her claim to the throne. Elizabeth replaced Catholic church leaders with Protestants, restored the church Articles and the Prayer Book of Edward VI, and took the title of 'supreme governor' – rather than head – of the Church of England, successfully locating a *via media* that has marked Anglicanism since that time.

As re-established by Elizabeth, the Anglican Church retained episcopal government and a set liturgy, offending many Calvinists, particularly refugees returning from Switzerland. Meanwhile Roman Catholics plotted and intrigued; every Catholic appeared a potential traitor since the pope had ordered them to overthrow Elizabeth.

SCOTLAND

DURHAM

NORTH SEA

Predominantly Protestant
Predominantly Catholic
Mixed religious allegiance
.... Boundaries of bishoprics
as re-formed by Henry VIII

Miles
0 10 20 30 40 50
0 10 20 30 40 50
Kilometers

Carlisle

CARLISLE

Durham

IRISH SEA

CHESTER

YORK

York

Humber R.

Chester

LINCOLN

Lincoln

BANGOR

ST ASAPH

LICHFIELD

Trent R.

BANGOR

Lichfield

ENGLAND

NORWICH

Norwich

ELY

1547 Martin Bucer professor
1552 Bucer helps create
radical 1552 Prayer Book

Severn R.

WALES

BANGOR

WORCESTER

PETERBOROUGH

Avon R.

HEREFORD

LINCOLN

Cambridge

ST DAVIDS

OXFORD

1555 Mary Tudor burns
Bishops Ridley & Latimer
1556 Mary burns
Archbishop Cranmer

LLANDAFF

GLOUCESTER

Oxford

LONDON

BRISTOL

SALISBURY

London

ROCHESTER

Becket's shrine
destroyed by
Protestants
in 1538

Wells

ROCHESTER CY.

BATH & WELLS

Salisbury

WINCHESTER

ROCHESTER

Canterbury

CANTERBURY

Avon R.

CHICHESTER

CY.

EXETER

BRISTOL

1549 Edward VI passes 1st Act of Uniformity: moderate Prayer Book
1552 Edward VI passes 2nd Act of Uniformity: radical Prayer Book, with 39 Articles
1554 Mary Tudor restores Roman Catholicism
1559 Elizabeth I makes moderate Protestant religious settlement

ENGLISH CHANNEL

Scotland was first awakened to Lutheranism by Patrick Hamilton (c. 1504–28), who had been attracted to Luther's writings as a student in Paris and later attended lectures at Wittenberg and the new university of Marburg. Charged in Scotland with heresy, Hamilton was burned at the stake. Many Protestant intellectuals now fled abroad, never to return. George Wishart (c. 1513–46) was martyred by the Scottish Catholic leader, Cardinal Beaton, who was later assassinated for his oppression of young reformers. Wishart's major contribution was his influence upon John Knox (c. 1514–72), who was to become leader of the Scottish Reformation.

Knox was taken prisoner by the French in 1547 and forced to serve as a galley slave. Upon his release, he played a part in English Reform as chaplain to Edward VI. During Mary Tudor's reign he fled to Geneva, where he was greatly influenced by Calvin.

In 1557 Scottish Protestants covenanted to bring about reform. Few of the population were Protestant, but this minority included important nobles such as the head of the Hamilton clan, and the Earls of Argyll, Glencairn, and Morton. These 'Lords of the Congregation' now summoned Knox from exile. After he preached against idolatry in Perth, iconoclasm swept across the nation. Knox continued to attack the papacy and the Mass in fiery sermons at St Giles' Cathedral, Edinburgh.

John Knox

Urged on by Knox, the dissident nobles seized churches and forced the French Regent, Mary of Guise, to take refuge in Edinburgh Castle. Backed by English forces, the rebels succeeded in enforcing Reform. At the request of the Scottish Parliament, Knox drew up a Confession of Faith and Doctrine (1560, replaced in 1647 by the Westminster Confession), emphasizing evangelical doctrine and urging the necessity of discipline. The Book of Discipline (1561) was followed by a new liturgy, the Book of Common Order (1564), and a translation of Calvin's Catechism. Knox had consolidated the Reformation in Scotland.

Mary Queen of Scots

In 1561 the unexpected return of Mary Stuart, Queen of Scots, re-ignited the religious issue. Mary had hoped to practise her Catholic faith in private while allowing Scotland to remain Protestant. Knox attacked Mary over her celebration of Mass at court and her dissolute entourage and personal life. Forced to abdicate in 1567, the queen finally lost Scotland for Roman Catholicism.

After the death of Knox, Protestant leadership passed to Andrew Melville (1545–1622), who became Principal of the University of Glasgow in 1574. Twice Moderator of the General Assembly, he strove to remove all traces of episcopacy in Scotland. Although Scotland had now embraced Presbyterian principles, for more than a century the Stuart monarchs continued to attempt to enforce episcopacy. Under royal pressure, pro-episcopal measures were adopted in 1584, but reversed in 1592. But James VI and his successors ultimately lost Scotland for the episcopal cause.

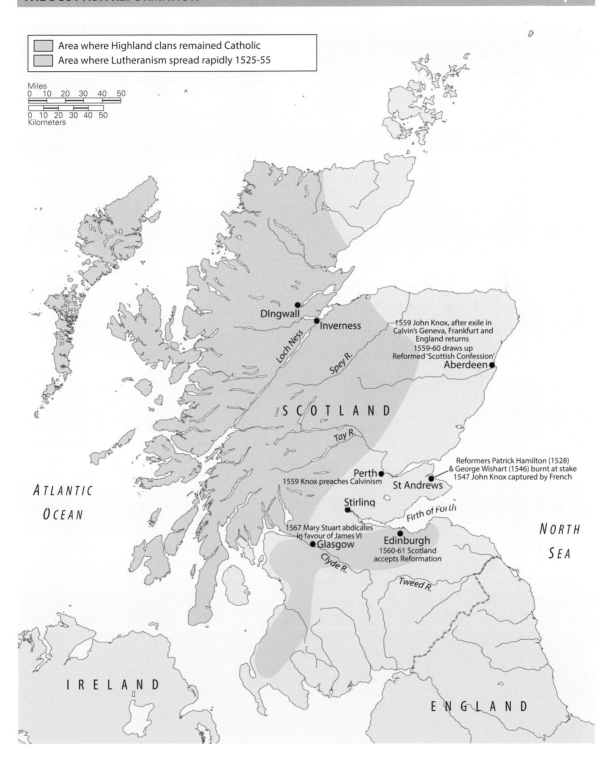

Area where Highland clans remained Catholic
Area where Lutheranism spread rapidly 1525-55

Miles
0 10 20 30 40 50
0 10 20 30 40 50
Kilometers

DIngwall

Inverness

Loch Ness

Spey R.

1559 John Knox, after exile in
Calvin's Geneva, Frankfurt and
England returns
1559-60 draws up
Reformed 'Scottish Confession'

Aberdeen

S C O T L A N D

Tay R.

Perth

1559 Knox preaches Calvinism

St Andrews

Reformers Patrick Hamilton (1528)
& George Wishart (1546) burnt at stake
1547 John Knox captured by French

Stirling

Firth of Forth

ATLANTIC
OCEAN

1567 Mary Stuart abdicates
in favour of James VI

Glasgow

Edinburgh

1560-61 Scotland
accepts Reformation

NORTH
SEA

Clyde R.

Tweed R.

IRELAND

ENGLAND

Reform in Poland

Poland had a strong tradition of anti-clericalism and of religious toleration. The Hussites had flourished in the west of the country in the fifteenth century and many Jews fled there from persecution in the west. In Lithuania there was even an Islamic Tatar population. But in 1500 the Roman Catholic Church remained dominant.

Reform first reached Poland in the 1520s when students from Wittenberg brought the message to Danzig and Krakow. It quickly gained popularity, mainly among German-speaking inhabitants of such major cities as Toruń and Elbląg. A Polish edition of Luther's *Small Catechism* was published in Königsberg in 1530.

The Duchy of Prussia, a Polish fief, emerged as key centre of reform, with a number of publishers issuing Bibles and catechisms in German, Polish, and Lithuanian. Lutheranism gained popularity particularly in the north.

Polish kings were either indifferent to Reform or believed religious disputes not to be royal business. Poland had a weak monarchy and the king lost further power as the nobility converted to Lutheranism. The king could do little without the cooperation of the Polish diet (*Sjem*), which was now dominated by reformist princes. In 1555 a diet suspended the jurisdiction of church courts, thereby giving legal recognition to Protestantism.

Calvinism

Calvinism proved particularly attractive to the nobility, mainly in Lesser Poland and the Grand Duchy of Lithuania. Sigismund II Augustus (r. 1548–72) was a friend of the Reformation and corresponded with Calvin. In 1563, the Brest Bible, the first complete Bible in Polish, was published. The most distinguished Polish theologian was the Calvinist John a Lasco (1499–1560), who later moved to England and helped shape the Reformation during the reign of Edward VI.

Poland also attracted other Protestant groupings, such as the Mennonites and Czech Brethren, the latter settling mainly in Greater Poland, around Leszno. A further reform group, the Polish Brethren, appeared in 1565, led among others by Fausto Sozzini (Faustus Socinus, 1539–1604), who denied the Trinity and the pre-existence of Christ. (In the seventeenth century 'Socinianism' was used as a pejorative term for Unitarians and other dissenters.) Other leading Polish Protestants included Mikołaj Rej (1505–69), 'father of Polish literature'; Marcin Czechowic (c. 1532–1613), a Socinian theologian; Andrzej Frycz Modrzewski (Andreas Fricius Modrevius, c. 1503–72), 'Father of Polish democracy'; and Symon Budny (c. 1530–93), a leader of the Polish Brethren.

Concord of Sandomir

In 1570 a general understanding was reached between Lutherans and Calvinists, expressed in the Concord of Sandomir, but this was marred by dissension over Socinianism. The Compact of Warsaw (1573) granted religious liberty to all, but this brief period of toleration ended under Sigismund III Vasa (r. 1587–1632).

Meanwhile neither the peasantry nor the poor had ever abandoned Catholicism. With the nobility becoming Protestant, the peasants and lesser nobility – who opposed the greater nobility and viewed the king as their ally – took the opposite religious viewpoint. Even where Protestantism was strong, a significant portion of the population remained Catholic.

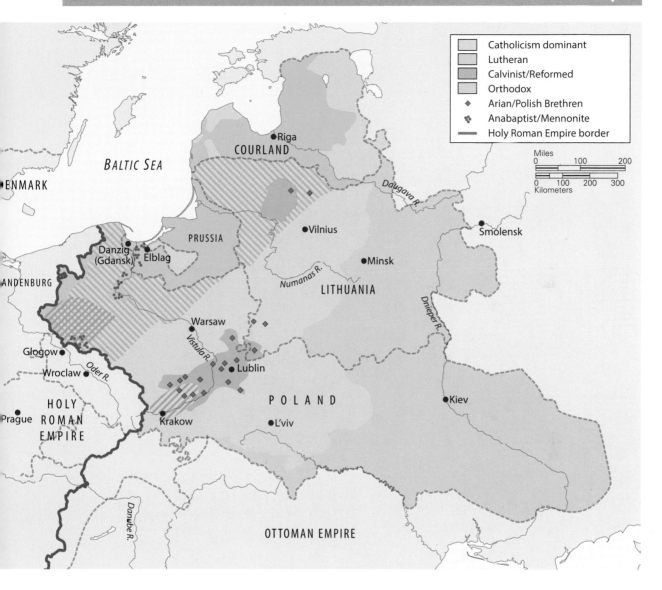

Legend	
	Catholicism dominant
	Lutheran
	Calvinist/Reformed
	Orthodox
♦	Arian/Polish Brethren
	Anabaptist/Mennonite
—	Holy Roman Empire border

Part 3

Catholic Reform and Counter-Reformation

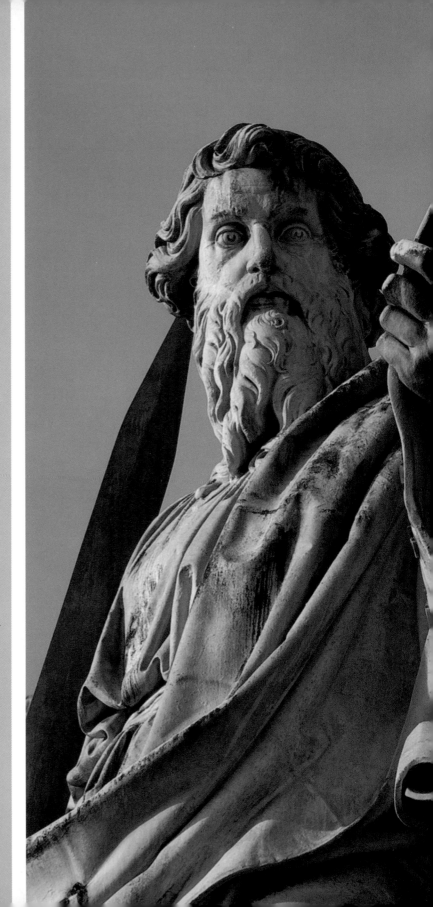

Go forth and set the
world on fire.

IGNATIUS OF LOYOLA

The situation within Western Europe had changed markedly by the time of the signing of the Peace of Augsburg (1555), which showed no real loss of land by the Lutherans, but a significant gain when compared with 1529.

In 1546 Charles V finally had the opportunity to move against the Lutherans, as had been his intention as far back as the Diet of Worms (1521). His long absence from Germany, caused by the revolt in Spain in the early 1520s and the threat from Francis I of France and Suleiman the Magnificent, was of huge advantage to the Reformation.

The ensuing Schmalkaldic War (1546–47) led to an attempt to settle the religious issues without a church council. This compromise – called an Interim – was acceptable to neither Protestants nor Catholics, and only the presence of Spanish occupation troops in northern Europe kept it in effect. Revolt, or the so-called War of Liberation, followed in which Maurice, Elector of Saxony, changed

sides, Henry II of France assisted against the Emperor, and Charles himself, having briefly enjoyed peace and almost universal victory, was forced to flee for safety through the snow-swept Alps.

Once Martin Luther had passed from the scene, a period of bitter theological warfare occurred within Protestantism. There was controversy over such matters as the difference between justification and sanctification; which doctrine was essential or non-essential; faith and works; and the nature of the 'real presence' at the Eucharist. This is the period of 'confessionalization', when Lutheranism developed a set system of beliefs and categories, defining it as a distinctive denomination or dogma – a development Luther had both foreseen and lamented. The *Book of Concord*, which sets out what we now understand as Lutheranism, was published in 1580. It included Melanchthon's Augsburg Confession and Augsburg Apology, Luther's two catechisms, the Schmalkaldic Articles drawn up in 1537, and the Formula of Concord. The dogmatism of some of the extreme Lutheran theologians now drove many people over to the Reformed or Calvinist church. Meanwhile the Reformed Christians in Germany adopted the *Heidelberg Confession* (1563) as their statement of faith.

Emperor Charles V.

Legend

- Catholic
- Lutheran
- Anglican
- Calvinist/Reformed
- Calvinist influenced
- Lutheran influenced
- Orthodox
- Muslim
- Anabaptist minorities
- Holy Roman Empire boundary
- Ottoman Empire boundary

NORTH SEA

NORWAY
Oslo

SWEDEN
Stockholm

SCOTLAND
Edinburgh

DENMARK
Copenhagen

BALTIC SEA

LIVONIA

COURLAND

PRUSSIA

LITHUANIA

Dublin
IRELAND

ENGLAND
WALES
London

Elbe R.

BRANDENBURG

Warsaw
POLAND

SPANISH NETHERLANDS
Antwerp

Wittenberg

Oder R.

Marburg

HOLY ROMAN EMPIRE

SILESIA

Rhine R.

Krakow

Paris

Strasbourg

Regensburg

BOHEMIA

MORAVIA

HUNGARY

Orleans

FRANCE

Basel

Vienna

AUSTRIA

Dneister R.

Danube R.

ATLANTIC OCEAN

SWISS CONFEDERATION

Trent

Lyons

Geneva

VENICE
Venice

Bordeaux

Rhône R.

GENOA
Genoa

Florence

PAPAL STATES

OTTOMAN EMPIRE
(MUSLIM MINORITY)

Toulouse

Ebro R.

Barcelona

Rome

NAPLES
Naples

PORTUGAL

Madrid

SPAIN

SARDINIA

bon

MEDITERRANEAN SEA

Palermo

SICILY

Miles
0   100   200   300

0   100 200   400
Kilometers

It has often been implied that the divide between the reforming Lutherans and Calvinists and the Church of Rome quickly became so wide and deep as to be unbridgeable. In fact there remained strong reforming pressures and groups within the Roman Catholic Church, often influenced by Humanist learning and a search for spirituality and renewal. A number of leaders in the Roman church were exploring ideas not dissimilar to those of Luther and the Protestant reformers, and many conferences and debates were held attempting to resolve differences and re-unite the church. Italy itself came much closer to turning Protestant than has usually been imagined.

After the excesses and corruption of some of the Renaissance popes, Pope Paul III (r. 1534–49) began to take steps to correct abuses and bring about renewal in the Roman Catholic Church. He appointed reformers to the College of Cardinals, set up a papal reform commission, and in 1545 convened the Council of Trent. Among the new cardinals created were Gasparo Contarini (1483–1542), Gian Pietro Carafa (later Paul IV, 1476–1559), Reginald Pole (1500–58), Jacopo Sadoleto (1477–1547), Pietro Bembo (1470–1547), and Jean du Bellay (c. 1493–1567). The papal reform commission that Paul appointed issued a formal report in 1537, and on its recommendation he reformed the papal bureaucracy, ordered an end to taking money for spiritual favours, and forbade the buying and selling of church appointments.

The Council of Trent

Paul III's most significant action was to call an ecumenical church council to deal with reform and the growing threat of Protestantism. As its venue he named the city of Trent (Trentino), just inside the area of the Italian peninsula ruled by the Emperor. His choice offended the French, who sent only a handful of church leaders to the council.

Delayed by the continuing conflict between Charles V and Francis I, the council came too late to re-unite Christian Europe; it could only reform, shore up, and define the polarization on the Roman Catholic side. For part of the period of the council's gestation and deliberations, the pope was formally at war with the Holy Roman Emperor, Charles V, or with his son, Philip II of Spain. By the time it convened, Lutheranism was already an organized body of doctrine, Strasbourg and Hesse were decided on their religious path, and Calvin well into his second period in Geneva.

Trent I

The council met in three main sessions: 1545–47, 1551–52, and 1562–63. It was not a continuous meeting, but in effect three separate gatherings attended by three different, but overlapping, groups of representatives of the Roman Church. Attendance was scanty and irregular for such a significant project, and on occasion feelings ran so high that physical fights broke out between delegates.

The first session opened with only four archbishops, twenty bishops, four generals of monastic orders, and a few theologians present – and without the lay princes to whom the Reformers looked for leadership. Some Catholic Humanist reformers attended – such as Reginald Pole – some of whom Protestants such as Bucer and Melanchthon had worked with previously at re-union meetings in 1540–41.

The Council's method of voting gave the pro-papal Italian bloc control. There was agreement that the Bible and tradition are equally valid sources of truth; the church alone can interpret the Bible authoritatively; and that Jerome's translation, the Vulgate, was normative. This made reconciliation

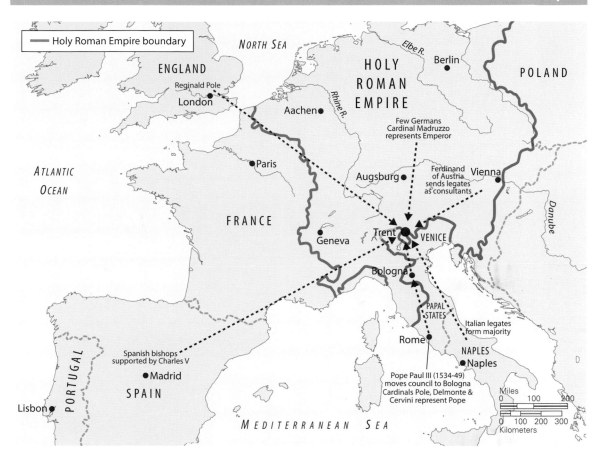

(Map labels: NORTH SEA, Elbe R., Berlin, POLAND, ENGLAND, HOLY ROMAN EMPIRE, Reginald Pole, London, Aachen, Rhine R., Few Germans Cardinal Madruzzo represents Emperor, ATLANTIC OCEAN, Paris, Augsburg, Ferdinand of Austria sends legates as consultants, Vienna, FRANCE, Geneva, Trent, VENICE, Danube, Bologna, Italian legates form majority, PAPAL STATES, PORTUGAL, Spanish bishops supported by Charles V, Madrid, SPAIN, Rome, NAPLES, Naples, Pope Paul III (1534-49) moves council to Bologna Cardinals Pole, Delmonte & Cervini represent Pope, Lisbon, MEDITERRANEAN SEA, Miles 0 100 200, Kilometers 0 100 200 300)

with Protestants impossible, since the Reformers asserted the primacy of the Bible, and the preacher's responsibility to interpret Scripture from the original texts. Decrees on justification, original sin, and the sacraments all strengthened the barrier between the churches.

Trent II

The largest number of delegates to attend the second session of the Council was fifty-nine. The Emperor held back the German bishops from this session until the pope agreed to allow Protestants to attend. Even then, the pope did not agree to the Emperor's demand that the Protestants be allowed to vote. As a result, no leading Lutheran theologians,

Reformed, or Calvinists came. However three delegations of Protestants arrived in late 1551, from Brandenburg, Württemberg, and Strasbourg, joined by representatives of Maurice of Saxony in 1552.

These Protestants called unsuccessfully for the re-opening of discussion on earlier council decisions. They also attempted to get the council to re-affirm the supremacy of a church General Council over the pope, as had been agreed at the Council of Basel (1431–49). Reckoning nothing would be gained by staying, the Protestants departed in March 1552. The inability or unwillingness of the two sides to reach any understanding illustrates the gulf between them.

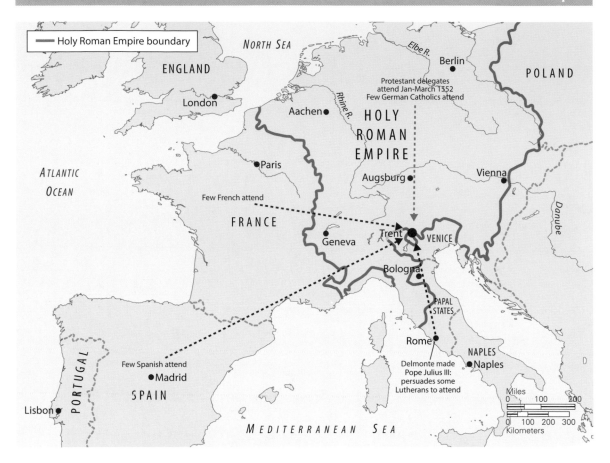

With little participation from France or Spain, and dominated by the Italian faction, the council condemned Calvinist, Zwinglian, and Lutheran views and reaffirmed the doctrine of transubstantiation.

Trent III

The Council did not meet at all during the papacy of the virulently anti-Protestant Paul IV (r. 1555–59), and the Jesuits dominated its third and final session. Present were two influential members of the Society of Jesus, Diego Laynez and Alfonso Salmerón.

This session was the best attended, with as many as 255 at one of its meetings, and the most productive. Substantial delegations

from Spain and France appeared, the latter sometimes at cross-purposes with the Italians. The Spanish were doctrinal hardliners, sensitive to the wishes of Charles V, who was also King Charles I of Spain.

A number of issues debated in earlier sessions were resolved. Medieval orthodoxy was reaffirmed for most of the doctrines under dispute in the Reformation. Transubstantiation, and established medieval practices connected with the Mass were all upheld. The seven sacraments were insisted upon, and celibacy of the clergy, the existence of purgatory, and indulgences all reaffirmed. However, the post of indulgence-seller was abolished and abuses linked to the

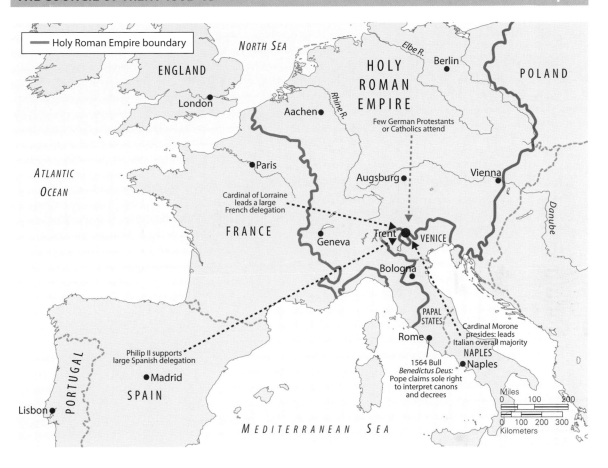

distribution of indulgences were condemned. The Council also increased papal authority by giving the pope the power to enforce the decrees of the council, and requiring church officials to promise him obedience. Important reforming measures were also passed on education, providing for the improved training of priests and for control of their conduct.

After the Council adjourned, its actions were confirmed and issued by Pope Pius IV in January 1564, along with his decisions on several issues that the Council had left unsettled. Scholastic-style theological definitions – with curses on anyone who did not agree with them – killed any

lingering Protestant hopes that church unity might be restored.

Trent ruled out any possibility of Christian reconciliation in the immediate future. But by re-elevating the papacy, by improving church organization, by dealing with the most glaring abuses pointed out by Protestant Reformers, and by clarifying doctrine and dogma, the Council of Trent gave the Church of Rome a clear position to uphold over the following centuries. The work of Trent stood the church in good stead during the wars of religion and the period of missionary expansion that lay ahead, providing a sense of renewed purpose and recovered morale.

Ignatius Loyola

Ignatius Loyola (c. 1491–1556), founder and leader of the Society of Jesus, is one of the most dramatic and influential figures in Christian history. He combined the spirituality of monasticism with the Crusaders' tradition of heroism in a disciplined programme for nurturing the individual soul and mind, and possessed a genius for charismatic and clear-headed leadership.

A Spanish nobleman, Ignatius was born in 1491 at the castle of Loyola, near the Pyrenees. He became a professional soldier, but in 1521 a leg wound cut short his military career. While recovering, he resolved to become a devoted follower of Jesus. Whereas Luther found peace by rejecting the traditions of the medieval church in favour of the basics of primitive Christianity, Loyola found peace by rededicating himself to the conventions of the medieval church.

Spiritual Exercises

Loyola travelled to the Montserrat Monastery, where he took monastic vows and hung up his arms in the chapel of the 'Black Madonna'. After temptations and agonies of soul that parallel Luther's – he spent a whole year (1522–23) in prayer and meditation – he was given Christian assurance in visions and trances. He worked on the first edition of his manual of self-discipline, *Spiritual Exercises*, and then made a pilgrimage to the Holy Land. His book, with its powerful appeal to the imagination and emphasis on obedience to Christ and to the Church of Rome, provided the cornerstone for the new ascetic order that Loyola founded.

Society of Jesus

Between 1524 and 1534 Loyola studied at Barcelona, Alcalá, Salamanca, and Paris, as he prepared to serve God. On 15 August 1534 he and six friends vowed to practise poverty, chastity, and celibacy, and to devote the rest of their lives to mission, initiating the 'Society of Jesus', popularly known as the Jesuits. They

Ignatius Loyola (c. 1491–1556).

NORTH SEA

Hamburg

Elbe R.

ENGLAND

Oxford

London

Rhine R.

HOLY
ROMAN
EMPIRE

Danube R.

Vienna

ATLANTIC
OCEAN

Seine R. Paris

⑥
1528-35 Studies at University
With companions,
including Francis Xavier,
takes vows

FRANCE

Milan●

VENICE

Venice●

① 1491 Born
1521-2 Spiritual conversion
whilst convalescent

Ferrara

③ 1552-3 Formulates
Spiritual Exercises

PAPAL
STATES

Rome●

Loyola●
GUIPUZCOA

Pamplona●

Xavier●

Manresa●

② Montserrat
1522 Claims vision of Mary

NAPLES

●Naples

SPAIN

Barcelona●

Salamanca●

●Alcalá

Madrid●

⑤ 1524-6 Studies at university
Suspected of belonging
to heretical *alumbrados*

④ 1523-4 Sails to Holy Land
Sent back by Franciscans

⑦
1539 forms Society of Jesus (Jesuits)
Loyola Superior-General
1540 Pope Paul III approves Jesuits
1556 dies

PORTUGAL

MEDITERRANEAN SEA

Miles
0   100   200   300

0   100 200   400
Kilometers

wanted to secure papal blessing to travel to the Holy Land, but this proved impossible as the Emperor, the pope, and Venice were all involved in attempting to break up an alliance between Francis I and Suleiman I.

In 1540 the new order received written authorization from Paul III and set out to accomplish its mission to carry the gospel to the peoples of newly discovered continents. The Jesuits regarded themselves as a new spiritual élite, at the pope's disposal to use however he thought appropriate for spreading the 'true church'. Absolute, unquestioning, military-style, obedience became its hallmark.

Rise of the Jesuits

When war between Venice and the Turks prevented their passage to Palestine, Ignatius Loyola and his six disciples began to work in north Italian cities. They gathered new recruits, sought direction from Pope Paul III, and elected Loyola as their general. In addition to the traditional vows of poverty, chastity, and obedience, the Jesuits insisted on an oath of absolute obedience to the pope. Every member of the Society was to obey the pope and the general of the order as unquestioningly 'as a corpse'.

The purpose of the society was to propagate the faith by every means at their disposal. Recruits had to be healthy, intelligent, and eloquent; no one of bad character or with unorthodox beliefs was admitted. The new order was highly centralized: its leaders were all appointed by the general, who was himself elected for life. It had no religious uniform, no bodily penances or fasts, and no choral recitation of the daily liturgy, which gave its members great flexibility compared with other orders, allowing them to become men of action. The Jesuit was expected to cultivate an inner life based on meditation and Loyola's *Spiritual Exercises*.

Although Loyola valued quality over quantity, the order grew rapidly, especially attracting the younger sons of noble families. When the founder died in 1556, there were already more than 1,500 Jesuits, mainly in Spain, Portugal, and Italy, but also in France, Germany, the Low Countries, India, Brazil, Japan, Africa, and almost every other country in Europe.

Three tasks

The Jesuits' work focussed on three main tasks: education, counteracting Protestantism, and missionary expansion into new areas. Education quickly became a major emphasis; within a decade the Jesuits had established a dozen colleges. Their schools soon became celebrated for their high standards and attainments, and many of the élite were won to Roman Catholicism by this means. A familiar Jesuit saying ran: 'Give me a child until he is

seven and he will remain a Catholic the rest of his life.'

Education was based on the *Plan of Studies* of 1599, which purified and simplified Renaissance Humanism. Philosophy in Jesuit schools generally followed Aristotle, while theology was adapted from Thomas Aquinas, for example in the system drawn up by Francisco Suarez (1548–1617), who taught at Alcalá and Coimbra.

Loyola did not found the Jesuits in order to combat Protestantism, but during the second half of the sixteenth century and throughout the seventeenth this increasingly became a Jesuit goal. In France, the Low Countries, southern Germany, and particularly in eastern Europe, the Jesuits led the counter-attack against Protestants. Using a variety of means, they recaptured large areas for the Church of Rome, earning a reputation as 'the feared and formidable storm-troops of the Counter Reformation' (Hillerbrand). Only in England did their campaign fail.

Several Jesuits served as papal representatives, or legates, in negotiations to tie countries such as Ireland, Sweden, and Russia more firmly to Rome. Other Jesuits served as court preacher or confessor to the Emperor, the kings of France and Poland, and the dukes of Bavaria. Peter Canisius (1521–97) from Nijmegen, in the Low Countries, an able preacher, apologist, and diplomat, became the most successful adversary of the Reformation in Germany and Poland. Robert Bellarmine (1542–1621) from Montepulciano, Tuscany, wrote catechisms and anti-Protestant works of theology that remained influential for centuries.

Legend:

- ■ Major Jesuit centre
- □ Major Jesuit centre with seminary
- ○ Jesuit seminary
- △ Jesuit school or other institution

- Area Catholic in 1560
- Catholic area lost to Protestantism after 1560
- Area regained by Catholicism by 1648
- Protestant
- Orthodox
- Muslim

NORTH SEA

SCOTLAND

BALTIC SEA

□Vilnius

IRELAND

ENGLAND

○Braunsberg

PRUSSIA

London

UNITED PROVINCES

HOLY ROMAN EMPIRE

POLAND

St Omer
Liège
Rouen
Rheims
Trier
○Mainz
○Fulda

Glatz

Prague □
Kuttenberg
Krumlau
Olmutz
Brno
■Krakow

Paris
1534 Jesuit movement starts
Pont-à-Mousson
Nancy
Dillingen
Molsheim
Ingolstadt
Founded 1549 Centre of Jesuits in Germany

○Trnava

La Flèche
Dôle
Bourges
SWISS CONFEDERATION
1562-3 Jesuits dominate 3rd session of Council
Vienna
Graz
Neuhaus

HUNGARY

FRANCE
Lyons

ATLANTIC OCEAN

△Padua

Bordeaux
Parma
Genoa

Avignon
Toulouse

1542 First Jesuit college founded by Andrea Lippomano

OTTOMAN EMPIRE

■Santiago de Compostela
Valladolid

Rome
1540 Jesuits recognized by Pope
ITALY
□Naples

■Salamanca
■Madrid
Toledo
■Valencia

PORTUGAL

SPAIN

bon

Palermo ■Messina
1548 First Jesuit school

■Seville

MEDITERRANEAN SEA

Trent

Miles
0 100 200 300

0 100 200 400
Kilometers

Francis Xavier

The courageous Jesuit missionary Francis Xavier (1506–52) towered above his peers as the 'apostle to the Indies and to Japan'. Xavier was born into the Spanish nobility in Navarre, Spain. In 1525, he went to study at the University of Paris, where he became one of the founding members of the Society of Jesus. When John III of Portugal asked the Jesuits for missionaries for his empire, Xavier responded, arriving in Goa, India, in May 1542. Admired for his ability to live and work alongside the poor, Francis soon moved on to Sri Lanka, the Molucca Islands, the Banda Islands, and the Malay Peninsula, preaching and baptizing wherever he went.

In August 1549, Xavier landed at Kagoshima, Japan, and – as in his previous missions – adapted to local mores to attract converts to establish a Christian community. He then sailed to Shangchuan ('St John's') Island, near Canton, but was unable to reach the mainland as it was closed to foreigners. Before Xavier could gain entry into China, fever incapacitated him, and in 1552 he died, aged only forty-six.

Statue of Francis Xavier and St Paul's Church, Malacca.

THE TRAVELS OF FRANCIS XAVIER

ATLANTIC OCEAN

EUR

FRANCE

SPAIN

PORTUGAL

1541 Departs on *Santiago* — ●Lisbon

AFRICA

ATLANTIC OCEAN

Miles
0   500   1000

0   500   1000   1500
Kilometers

map 41

JAPAN

1550-51
Yamaguchi

1549
Kagoshima

ASIA

CHINA

December 1552
Dies of fever

1549
Canton

Shangchuan

PACIFIC
OCEAN

INDIA

Bombay

SOCOTRA

May 1542,1548,
1552 leaves for China
on *Santa Cruz*

Goa

St Thomas

Cape Comorin

SRI LANKA

Oct 1542-1545
Remains in South India
& Sri Lanka

1544,1546-7,
1549,1551
Malacca

SUMATRA

BORNEO

1546
Maluku Islands:
Amboin, Ternate,
Baranura, Morotai

MOLUCCAS

elinde

ZANZIBAR

INDIAN OCEAN

lozambique
41-42
stays
onths

AUSTRALIA

Catholic Missions to America

Following Pope Alexander VI's line of demarcation, the Portuguese colonized Brazil while the remainder of Latin America fell within the Spanish sphere of influence.

Columbus landed in the West Indies in the same year that the Spanish drove the Moors out of their last stronghold in Spain, and his companions brought the same crusading zeal to the New World. Combining a desire for wealth and military success with dedication to Christian mission, they created a huge Spanish empire in the Americas. Although the men who led Spain's conquest of Latin America were often cruel and used questionable means to achieve their objectives, they saw themselves as fulfilling a mission to liberate the natives from superstitious practices. Hernán Cortes (1485–1547), who led the conquest of Mexico, attended Mass daily, carried a statue of the Virgin Mary with him wherever he went, and displayed the cross on the flag he carried.

Using brutal methods, the Spanish conquered the Aztec kingdom in Mexico and the Incas of Peru. Cortes slaughtered more than 3,000 Cholula in Mexico, and in 1532 Francisco Pizarro (c. 1471/76–1541), the conqueror of Peru, massacred thousands of Incas. The Inca leader was sentenced to death by burning at the stake; but when he agreed to be baptized, his sentence was commuted to death by strangling.

The conquest of Mexico and Peru provided Spain with a rich source of precious metals and vast tracts of land which were granted to Spanish settlers. In return for providing protection and instruction in the Christian faith, the landowners were allowed to use the natives as virtual slaves. Although Queen Isabella of Spain forbade enslavement of the

map 42

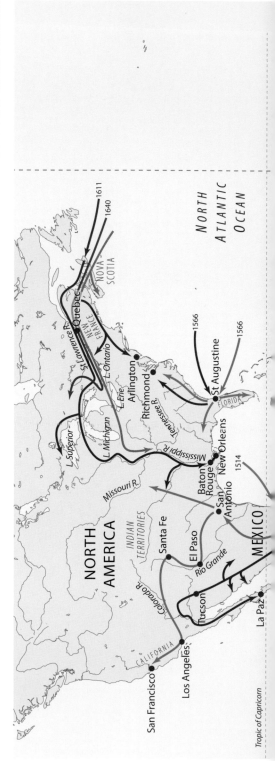

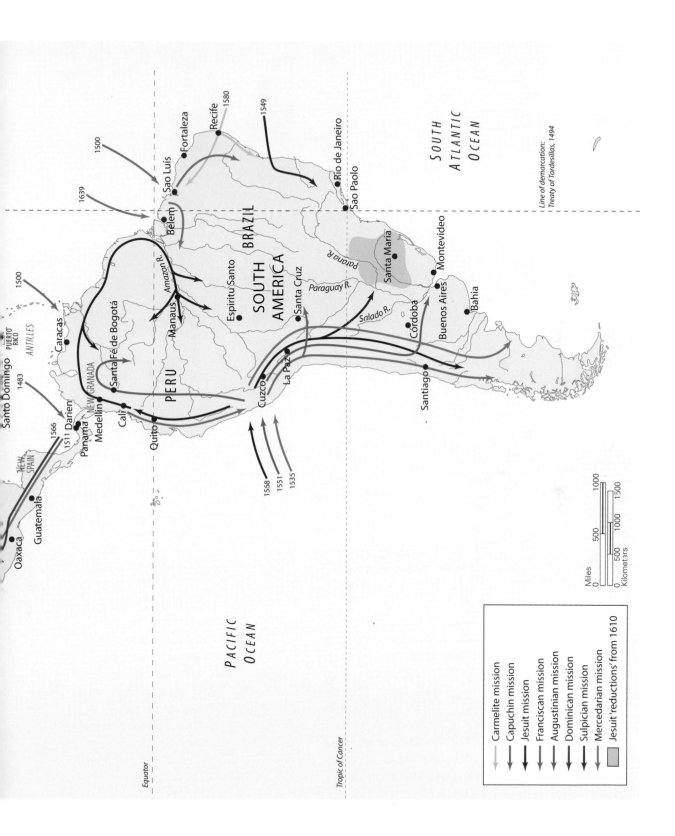

SOUTH
AMERICA

BRAZIL

PERU

NEW
GRANADA

NEW
SPAIN

ANTILLES

PUERTO
RICO

SOUTH
ATLANTIC
OCEAN

PACIFIC
OCEAN

Equator

Tropic of Cancer

Line of demarcation:
Treaty of Tordesillas, 1494

Amazon R.
Paraná R.
Paraguay R.
Salado R.

Santo Domingo
Oaxaca
Guatemala
Panama
Darien
Medellin
Cali
Quito
Caracas
Santa Fé de Bogotá
Belém
Manaus
Espiritu Santo
São Luis
Fortaleza
Recife
São Paolo
Rio de Janeiro
Santa Maria
Montevideo
Bahia
Buenos Aires
Cordoba
Santiago
La Paz
Santa Cruz
Cuzco

1483
1511
1566
1500
1500
1639
1580
1500
1549
1558
1551
1535

Miles
0   500   1000
Kilometers
0   500   1000   1500

Carmelite mission
Capuchin mission
Jesuit mission
Franciscan mission
Augustinian mission
Dominican mission
Sulpician mission
Mercedarian mission
Jesuit 'reductions' from 1610

Statue of Francisco Pizarro, Trujillo, Caceres, Spain.

native population and Emperor Charles V attempted to protect their rights, the colonists ignored the rules laid down by the distant government. In view of the appalling way in which they were treated, it is surprising many Native Americans did convert to Christianity: it was claimed more than one million were baptized between 1524 and 1531. However, clearly enthusiastic missionaries overestimated their success. Moreover conversion was often superficial; many 'converts' had minimal understanding of their new faith. Frequently the result was syncretism, with pre-Christian practices and beliefs surviving and mingling with Christian tradition.

Generally the Spanish treated the natives as inferior, and although in 1536 one bishop founded a college to train native priests near Mexico City, the Spanish laity repudiated the concept of native clergy. A few Spanish priests protested, best known of whom was Bartolomé de Las Casas (1484–1566), whose father had sailed with Columbus on his second voyage. De Las Casas became convinced the current treatment of Native Americans was evil and

contrary to Christian teaching, and from 1514 he spent his life campaigning for their rights. He worked tirelessly in Spain and the Spanish colonies to improve conditions for Native Americans, often encountering fierce opposition. A few other priests and laymen also came to the natives' defence.

Jesuit missions

As they went to America, Africa, and Asia in search of converts, Jesuit priests often travelled in Spanish and Portuguese ships in search of new colonies and new riches. They endowed their converts with their own enthusiastic brand of Catholicism. The Jesuits played a leading role in the conversion of Brazil and Paraguay, and, with the Dominicans, Franciscans, and Augustinians, led the Church of Rome in a period of rapid overseas expansion between 1550 and 1650. Almost all of Mexico, Central and South America, along with a large part of the population of the Philippines, became adherents of the Roman Catholic Church by these means at this time.

The Jesuits introduced a controversial method of protecting Native Americans from exploitation. Between 1583 and 1605 they created a system of self-sufficient native reservations that offered a settlement and refuge for the Guarani Indians of Paraguay and Brazil who had been enslaved by the Spanish colonists. Although colonists opposed this policy, Philip III of Spain aided the Jesuits by means of subsidies and legal measures. This venture later became so successful that the Spanish government no longer needed to subsidize it.

The Jesuits set up around thirty of these reservations, known as 'Reductions', which included hospitals, schools, and provision for entertainment and work. Sites for these Reductions were chosen for their healthy climate and proximity to water, and planned on a square pattern with the church at the centre. Residents led a rather regimented life, separated from the 'corruption' of the wider society, in a system that has been criticized for its paternalism and regimentation.

JESUIT REDUCTIONS IN PARAGUAY   map 43

By 1555 there was a Reformed church in Paris, and five years later more than seventy Protestant congregations in France. From the late 1550s the French Protestants, who included many from the rich nobility and merchant and manufacturing middle classes, became known as 'Huguenots'. In 1559 a Protestant General Synod met and adopted a strongly Calvinistic confession of faith.

In an attempt to reconcile French Protestants and Roman Catholics, a Colloquy was held in 1561 at Poissy, near Paris, led on the Catholic side by Cardinal François de Tournon (1489–1562), and on the Huguenot side by Theodore Beza and Peter Martyr Vermigli; but it failed in its aims.

Between 1562 and 1598 a series of eight civil wars raged intermittently in a struggle for power between the Huguenots and Roman Catholics. A brief lull followed the Peace of St Germain (1570), which granted the nobility freedom of worship, allowed Huguenots two places of worship in each district of France, and put four cities – Cognac, La Charité, Montauban, and La Rochelle – under Huguenot control.

St Bartholomew's Day massacre

But on St Bartholomew's Day 1572, Huguenots in Paris and elsewhere were massacred in cold blood, a blow that shattered – but did not destroy – Protestantism in France. When the Protestant Henry IV succeeded to the French throne in 1589, Protestant hopes ran high; but French Catholics formed an alliance with the King of Spain and threatened to plunge the country in blood if he remained a Protestant. Henry yielded for the sake of peace and to preserve his throne: he is falsely supposed to have claimed, 'Paris is well worth a Mass.'

After further devastation, and with all parties exhausted, a compromise was reached in the Edict of Nantes of 1598. This gave Huguenots the right to public office and public worship except in Paris, Rheims, Toulouse, Lyons, and Dijon; and a number of cities were listed as Protestant 'places of refuge'. Meanwhile Roman Catholicism remained the official religion of the realm, now followed by a majority of the population.

Edict of Nantes

The Edict of Nantes compromise endured precariously until revoked by King Louis XIV (1643–1715) in 1685, for which action the Jesuits were partly responsible. This caused hundreds of Protestants to reconvert to Catholicism and thousands more to flee the country. Many Huguenots made their way to Geneva, the Netherlands, Prussia, England, and North America; others remained and suffered persecution or fled to the mountains of central France in an attempt to avoid it.

map 44

WALES

ENGLAND

NORTH SEA

London

Canterbury

Southampton

Winchelsea

Rye

ENGLISH CHANNEL

NETHERLANDS

Legend:
- ▲ Major Huguenot church c.1580
- ● Huguenot church c. 1580
- ■ Huguenot stronghold
- ○ Concentration of Huguenot refugees
- ▼ St Bartholomew's Day and subsequent massacres
- Controlled by Huguenots in 1598
- Part controlled by Huguenots in 1598

PICARDY

Rouen

Sedan

HOLY ROMAN EMPIRE

Jersey

Seine R.

1561 Colloquy fails to reconcile
Catholics and Protestants

NORMANDY

Poissy

Meaux

Paris

BRITTANY

1572 Massacre of Protestants
on St Bartholomew's Day
1594 Henry IV reverts to Catholicism

Troyes

Loire R.

1598 Edict temporarily
ends religious conflict

Angers

BURGUNDY

Saumur

Bourges

La Charité

Neuchâtel

Nantes

POITOU

SWISS
CONFEDERATION

1627-8 After siege
Huguenots subjugated

La Rochelle

Geneva

Cognac

Lyons

SAVOY

ATLANTIC OCEAN

FRANCE

AUVERGNE

Rhône R.

Grenoble

Turin

DAUPHINÉ

Bordeaux

○Orange

Albi

Avignon

Montauban

Gaillac

Montpellier

PROVENCE

GASCONY

Pau

Toulouse

LANGUEDOC

1562, 1569
Catholics massacre
Protestants after attempt
to seize city

San Sebastian

Marseille

NAVARRE

MEDITERRANEAN SEA

SPAIN

Miles
0   50   100

0   50   100   150
Kilometers

Netherlands Reform

For 600 years the Low Countries had belonged to a middle kingdom between the Frankish and Germanic powers – most recently Burgundy. The region was divided into seventeen autonomous provinces: those in the northern provinces spoke Flemish or Dutch, while the Walloons, in the southern provinces, spoke a dialect of French. United under the Duke of Burgundy, the people possessed a strong sense of independence.

The earliest Protestants in the Netherlands were Lutherans, soon followed by Anabaptists. After the fall of the radical outpost of Münster, the peaceable Mennonites became the dominant Anabaptist group in the Low Countries.

In 1509, Charles V, himself born in the Low Countries, became Duke of Burgundy. Initially he reacted to religious diversity with suppression: between 1518 and 1528 around 400 people were sentenced for religious dissent. The first to be burned were two Lutherans in 1523, but such persecution was unpopular even among Catholics. Local authorities were reluctant to enforce the laws against heresy and people sometimes rose locally in protest against executions.

Calvinism

In the 1550s Calvinism began to appear. Guido de Bres (or Guy de Bray, 1522–67), a French-speaking minister trained in Geneva, drafted the Belgic Confession in 1561; this was accepted by a Synod in Antwerp in 1566, and at Dort in 1619. In 1574 the University of Leiden was founded to promote Reformed theology.

The Belgic Confession was presented to the new ruler of the Netherlands, Philip II of Spain, with an affirmation of loyalty. However he was fiercely committed to Roman Catholicism and unwilling to make concessions to heretics. Philip persisted in persecution even when it was clear he was alienating his subjects. Determined as he was to stamp out heresy and curb the independent spirit of the Low Countries, war inevitably resulted.

Revolt against Spain

The religious war that ensued was largely a revolt against Spain, led by the Counts of Egmont and Horn and William of Orange ('William the Silent', 1533–84). In 1566 iconoclastic riots broke out across the Low Countries, as zealous Protestants attacked churches and monasteries and destroyed images. Philip had withdrawn to Spain, and after his sister, the regent, Margaret of Parma, made some religious concessions, the Protestants and Orange, Egmont, and Horn helped restore order. From April 1566 to April 1567 there was a brief respite in persecution – the 'wonder year' – during which Protestantism prospered and grew significantly.

But in 1567 Philip II took his revenge, sending the brutal Duke of Alba (or Alva) with 10,000 troops to commence a reign of terror. Egmont and Horn, who had earlier helped suppress the riots and declared their loyalty to Philip, were publicly executed and soon celebrated as martyrs. Between 6,000 and 8,000 people suspected of heresy were brought before the 'Council of Troubles' – known by the rebels as the 'Council of Blood' – and many of them executed. Penal taxation was imposed and local autonomy suppressed. Many Protestants fled to neighbouring countries.

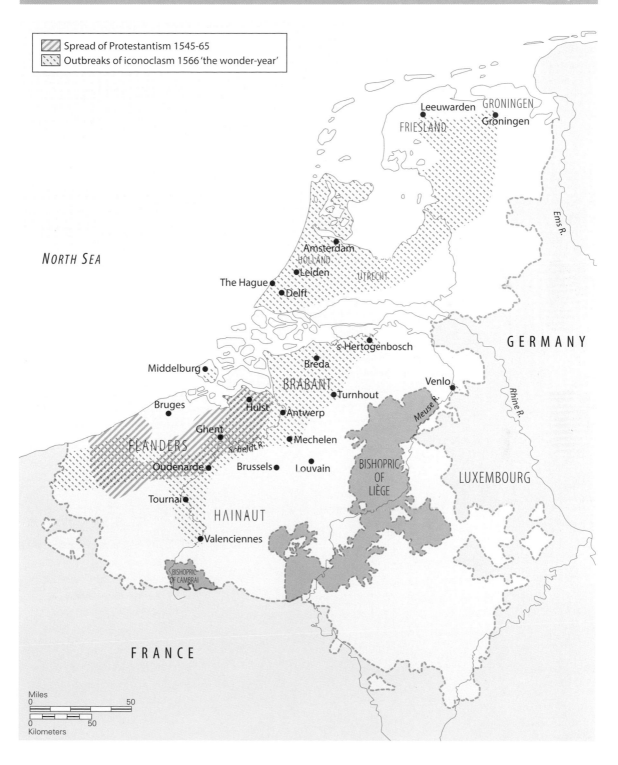

Spread of Protestantism 1545-65
Outbreaks of iconoclasm 1566 'the wonder-year'

GRONINGEN

Leeuwarden   Groningen

FRIESLAND

NORTH SEA

Amsterdam
HOLLAND
Leiden
The Hague   UTRECHT
Delft

GERMANY

Ems R.

Rhine R.

's-Hertogenbosch

Middelburg   Breda

BRABANT   Venlo

Turnhout

Meuse R.

Bruges   Hulst   Antwerp

Ghent   Mechelen

FLANDERS   Scheldt R.   BISHOPRIC
OF
LIÈGE   LUXEMBOURG

Oudenarde   Brussels   Louvain

Tournai

HAINAUT

Valenciennes

BISHOPRIC
OF
CAMBRAI

FRANCE

Miles
0   50

0   50
Kilometers

William the Silent emerged as the hero of the struggle with Spain, finding his strongest support in the northern provinces of Holland, Zeeland, and Utrecht, where Calvinism had made significant gains. In 1572 his 'sea beggars' captured a number of ports and defeated the Spanish fleet in the Zuider Zee. The rebels even opened the dikes to hinder the invading Spanish army. Philip II was never able to regain the northern provinces and by 1577 had lost most of the Low Countries.

The 'Spanish Fury' – when the unpaid Spanish troops in the southern provinces sacked Antwerp and murdered up to 8,000 of its inhabitants – enraged the people of the southern provinces and in November 1576 they joined the northern provinces in a treaty known as the Pacification of Ghent. The following year all the provinces joined in the Union of Brussels; people of both confessions combined to resist the Spanish tyranny.

The Spanish cause was rescued by a new commander, the Duke of Parma, who arrived with 20,000 troops in 1578. Victorious on the battlefield, he regained the loyalty of the southern provinces in 1579 by the Union of Arras. In response, the northern provinces of Holland, Zeeland, Utrecht, Gelderland, Friesland, Overijssel, and Groningen joined in the Union of Utrecht, by which they committed themselves to freedom of conscience for all citizens. In 1581 the States-General of the northern provinces proclaimed the independence of the United Provinces of the Dutch Republic.

William the Silent was assassinated in 1584, at a time when Parma was successfully regaining much territory, putting the Protestant cause in jeopardy. However the Dutch Protestants now produced two able new leaders: Johan van Oldenbarnevelt and Maurice of Nassau. The latter recovered many of the towns Parma had captured, and by 1600 had effectively blocked any further advance from the southern provinces.

Low Countries divided

In 1609 the new ruler of Spain, Philip III, signed a Twelve Years' Truce that recognized the division of the Low Countries into the Catholic southern provinces and the Protestant north.

War recommenced in 1621, but now the Dutch held all the advantages. Their armies pushed the Spanish forces south and their fleet enjoyed great success. By the Peace of Westphalia (1648), Spain finally recognized the independence of the United Provinces.

Reformed Church

Although the Calvinists played a major role in gaining independence from Spain, their ministers did not manage to turn the Netherlands into a new Geneva. The Reformed Church became the 'public' church in the sense that it was the only church the secular authorities recognized, but Remonstrants (followers of the theology of Arminius), Mennonites, and Lutherans were all allowed to hold services in their homes, and even Roman Catholic house-churches were not harassed. However in the southern provinces, Catholicism was restored and the remnants of Protestantism suppressed, in what now became known as the Spanish Netherlands.

Legend:
- United Provinces
- Spanish Netherlands
- Disputed areas
- Church lands
- Approximate linguistic boundary
- Town with early Lutheran concentration
- Town with early Calvinist/Reformed concentration
- Town with early Anabaptist concentration

1550s Dutch and English exiles publish many Protestant titles
1571 Synod agrees Reformed Presbyterian order for Dutch Protestants

Emden

GRONINGEN
Leeuwarden
Groningen
FRIESLAND

DRENTHE

Zwolle
ZUIDERZEE

Egmont

1579 Seven northern provinces
in Union of Utrecht declare
independence of Spain

OVERIJSSEL

Harlem
Amsterdam
Deventer

NORTH SEA

HOLLAND
GELDERLAND
Zutphen

1584 William of Orange
assassinated

The Hague
Woerden
UTRECHT
Utrecht
ZUTPHEN

1572 Protestant 'Sea Beggars'
set off rebellion against Alva

Delft

Brill
Dort

GERMANY

ZEELAND

UPPER
GELDERLAND

1568 Protestants flee persecution to
Emden and the Palatinate

Breda

Rhine R.

Bruges

Antwerp

BRABANT

Meuse R.

BISHOPRIC
OF
LIÈGE

Cologne

Ghent

FLANDERS

Scheldt R.

1585 Spain reconquers
Southern Netherlands after revolt

Maastricht

Calais

Ypres

Brussels

FLEMISH

WALLOON

Tournai

NAMUR

ARTOIS

Douai

HAINAUT

Namur

Arras

Valenciennes

1579
Catholic provinces form
Union of Arras loyal to
Philip II of Spain

Cambrai
BISHOPRIC
OF CAMBRAI

LUXEMBOURG

Moselle R.

1567 Philip II of Spain sends
Duke of Alva to suppress Protestants

Luxembourg

FRANCE

Miles
0   50

0   50
Kilometers

Ems R.

Philip II formed his *Grande y Felicísima Armada* ('Great and Most Happy Navy') to respond to challenges to his Roman Catholic faith and his pride as King of Spain and Naples (from 1556) and Portugal (from 1580), and ruler of half the Habsburg lands plus the rich Spanish Empire in the New World. Convinced of his crusade to re-establish Catholic Christendom, he had ruthlessly put down the final revolt of the Moriscos – secret Moorish Muslims who had outwardly conformed to Catholicism (1569–71) – and won the critical Battle of Lepanto (7 October 1571), sinking 80 Turkish galleys and capturing 130 others.

Philip had been vacillating about an attack on England, which was proving a constant irritant. The English were assisting the Dutch rebels, raiding Philip's convoys from New Spain, defying the pope, and obedient to an excommunicated queen – Elizabeth. Finally, in 1587, England executed the Catholic Mary Stuart, Queen of Scots, who had been forced into exile by John Knox and other Protestant leaders.

In July 1588 Philip despatched the mighty Armada to conquer England and restore it to Roman Catholicism. The military force he assembled was among the largest ever gathered for a sea attack, consisting of 132 ships, 18,000 soldiers, 7,000 sailors, and 3,165 cannon. In addition Philip planned to pick up in Calais 17,000 battle-hardened troops under the command of the Duke of Parma, creating what seemed like an invincible force for the invasion of England. Once his troops had landed, Philip also expected Roman Catholics in England to rise up against their heretical queen.

Disaster

Facing a threat that might have brought an end to Protestantism, England waited in fear. But everything went wrong for the Spanish. Bad planning, poor communications, excellent English seamanship under Sir Francis Drake, Sir John Hawkins, and Lord Howard of Effingham, and a 'Protestant wind' that blew the Spanish ships away from the English coast brought disaster to the Armada. Its ruin was completed by wild storms that drove the unwieldy Spanish galleons ashore as they sailed on around the British Isles.

This famous victory continued to be celebrated long after Elizabeth's death, and in the following century provided material for Protestant preachers to demonstrate that the English were a 'chosen people'. Although English Roman Catholics remained loyal throughout the crisis, they nevertheless became identified with the threat from Spain.

Philip II of Spain.

Route of Armada
Battle
Ships sunk
Realms of Philip II

Shetland Is.

August - December 1588
19 ships destroyed by storms

Orkney Is.

NORWAY

NORTH
SEA

SWEDEN

Hebrides

Aberdeen

SCOTLAND

Admiral Howard calls off chase

DENMARK

BALTIC
SEA

Edinburgh

Some Spanish
reach land

IRELAND

ENGLAND

English prevent
Spanish anchoring

Blockaded
by Dutch

Amsterdam

WALES

London

Antwerp

SPANISH NETHERLANDS

HOLY
ROMAN
EMPIRE

21 July
English attack:
2 Spanish ships
abandoned

Bristol

Solent

Bruges

Plymouth

Portland

Dunkirk

Parma's army of 30,000
waits to invade England

Lizard

ENGLISH CHANNEL

Gravelines

Elbe R.

Oder R.

19 July
Medina-Sidonia
sees land

21 July
English attack

Le Havre

8 August English beat Spanish fleet
Plan to join with Parma defeated

Rhine R.

ATLANTIC
OCEAN

Brest

Calais roads
27 July
Spanish anchor to meet Parma's land force
28 July
English fireships scatter Spanish fleet

Danube R.

FRANCE

Winter 1588
67 Spanish
ships return

Rhône R.

12 July 1588
Armada sails again

Corunna

Santander

May-July 1588
Armada dispersed
in storm

Ebro R.

SPAIN

Barcelona

NAPLES

Madrid

SARDINIA

PORTUGAL

Lisbon

Cadiz

MEDITERRANEAN SEA

SICILY

87 Francis Drake destroys Spanish ships
May 1588 Armada sets sail

Miles
0   100   200   300

0   100 200   400
Kilometers

THE SPANISH ARMADA   119

Part 4

Early Modern Europe

The towers stand in flames,
the church is violated.
The strong are massacred …
fire, pestilence and death
my heart have dominated.

ANDREAS GRYPHIUS, 1636

During the 1540s and early 1550s, English-style religious changes were cautiously introduced in Ireland, guided by the experienced Lord Deputy, Sir Anthony St Leger, who was personally no enthusiast for Protestantism. Most Irish bishops accepted the oath of royal supremacy to Henry VIII, and under Edward VI the government secured widespread use of the 1549 Book of Common Prayer. Only in the far north – in the remote and predominantly Gaelic parts of the Archdiocese of Armagh – was there no religious innovation.

Mary Tudor's restoration of traditional religion was enthusiastically welcomed in Ireland. She began to plant immigrant 'New English' settlers in the midland areas of King's County and Queen's County (Offaly and Leix), and Queen Elizabeth promoted further plantation schemes.

Plantation

This New English plantation strategy made it easy for the Irish to regard all incoming Englishmen as enemies and provoked serious warfare in the 1570s and 1590s. The Gaelic aristocracy allied with agents of the Counter-Reformation and with England's Catholic enemies – principally Spain, which made repeated but unsuccessful efforts to aid Irish Catholics. The Catholics now began to reshape Irish traditionalist religion and by the 1580s younger Irish clergy were increasingly choosing allegiance to the Pope rather than to the Queen.

Thousands of Irish left for Catholic Spain or France, either permanently or to get a non-Protestant education. Between 1590 and 1649, six colleges were set up in Spain and Portugal with the main purpose of training Irish clergy. These clergy returned to share the popularity of the mendicant Orders, whose communal life had continued unbroken in many parts of western Ireland, often still in their original buildings. Only a handful of major Irish towns established anything like a 'well-regulated' English Protestant parish, although the foundation of Trinity College, Dublin, in 1594 offered an education for the new Protestant governing class.

Scots settlers

Previously the strongest Gaelic region of Ireland, the most extensive plantation scheme was implemented in Ulster. From 1609 James I backed projects to import settlers, mostly from the lawless border areas of Scotland. These new arrivals were not always convinced Protestants, but characteristically professed Protestantism when a land-grabbing scheme backed by Protestant money from the city of London was implemented. Throughout Ireland, New English settlers, often holding a Calvinist theology that portrayed them as God's chosen people living among barbarous papists, came to dominate the established Church of Ireland.

In 1597 the Jesuits arrived permanently in Ireland, and by the 1620s Roman Catholics had about the same number of clergy working in the island as the Protestants. The Counter-Reformation achieved one of its greatest victories in Ireland: official Protestantism became an elite sect and Roman Catholicism the popular religion, a result unique in the Reformation.

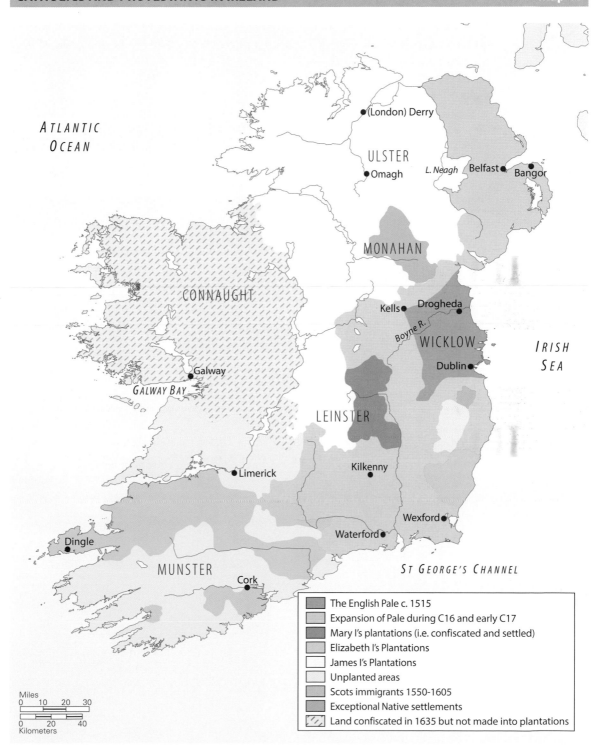

ATLANTIC
OCEAN

(London) Derry

ULSER

Omagh

L. Neagh　Belfast　Bangor

MONAHAN

CONNAUGHT

Kells　Drogheda

Boyne R.

WICKLOW

Dublin

IRISH
SEA

Galway

GALWAY BAY

LEINSTER

Limerick

Kilkenny

Wexford

Waterford

ST GEORGE'S CHANNEL

Dingle

MUNSTER

Cork

Miles
0　10　20　30

0　　20　　40
Kilometers

▨	The English Pale c. 1515
▨	Expansion of Pale during C16 and early C17
▨	Mary I's plantations (i.e. confiscated and settled)
▨	Elizabeth I's Plantations
☐	James I's Plantations
▨	Unplanted areas
▨	Scots immigrants 1550-1605
▨	Exceptional Native settlements
▨	Land confiscated in 1635 but not made into plantations

Early in the seventeenth century, Protestants began to colonize North America, starting with settlements on the Atlantic coast. One of the powerful side-effects of the Reformation was to give oppressed people a spiritual motive for emigration. The first colonists combined missionary zeal with a desire for freedom of worship, while they also often had commercial motives.

Following early colonization attempts by explorers such as Sir Humphrey Gilbert and Sir Richard Grenville, in 1607 a community was set up at Jamestown, Virginia, with Robert Hunt acting as Anglican chaplain. However Anglicanism was never popular in Virginia or the other colonies. The church authorities failed to provide a bishop for New England, which tended to weaken the Episcopalian church during the colonial period.

Some of the migration originated in expatriate English nonconformist and Separatist communities in the Netherlands that had set up churches there since the 1590s. The Pilgrim Fathers who disembarked at Plymouth, New England, in 1620, were Independents who had already left the English national church to seek ecclesiastical asylum in Holland.

James I

King James I made some attempt to reconcile Puritan clergy, who had been alienated by the blocking of further reform in the Church of England. But after Charles I succeeded him in 1625, religious conflict worsened and Parliament increasingly questioned the king's authority.

Replica of the Pilgrim Fathers' vessel *Mayflower* off Massachusetts, New England.

In 1629, Charles dissolved Parliament, in an attempt to neutralize his enemies there, who included many Puritan laymen.

With such a hostile religious and political climate, many Puritans decided to leave the country. The 'Great Migration' of 1629–40 saw 80,000 people leave England,

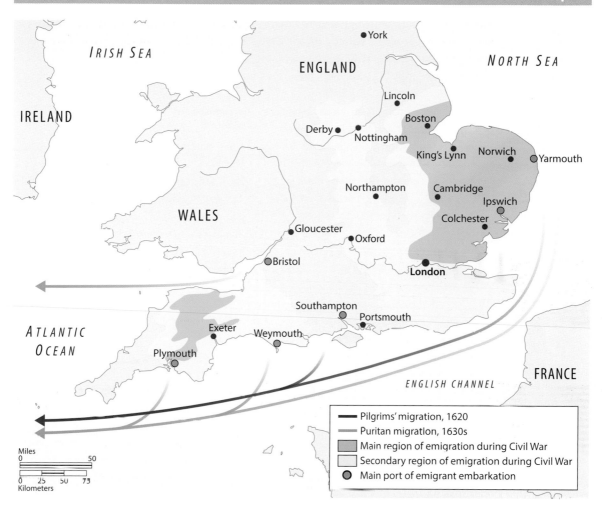

with some 20,000 migrating to each of Ireland, New England, the West Indies, and the Netherlands. The 'Winthrop fleet' of eleven ships, led by the flagship *Arbella* (or *Arabella*), took around 800 passengers to the Massachusetts Bay Colony in 1630. Immigrants to New England came from every English county except Westmoreland, with almost half from Norfolk, Suffolk, and Essex. By 1641, 200 ships had arrived with around 21,000 immigrants, among them 129 clergymen and theologians with links to Cambridge University, especially Emmanuel College, and to East Anglia, where many had held parishes or had family connections. The movement of colonists to New England was mainly of families with some education leading quite prosperous lives.

Migration continued until Parliament was finally recalled in 1640, when it dropped off. When the English Civil War began in 1641, some colonists returned to England to fight on the Puritan side. Possibly 7 to 11 percent of colonists returned to England after 1640, including about one-third of the clergymen.

Christian Europe 1600

In the late sixteenth and early seventeenth centuries, wars of religion shook every country in Europe. These conflicts also involved other volatile forces: the rise of nationalism, competition between aristocratic families, conflicts between monarchs and ambitious nobles, and the decay of imperial authority. In Germany all these forces were present, and the situation was complicated by the large number of small states and principalities that survived from the feudal age.

The Peace of Augsburg (1555) merely provided a breathing space. The territorial expansion of Protestantism reached its widest extent in central Europe around 1566, and then began to recede before the militant forces of the Counter-Reformation. A Protestant 'Union' of 1608 was countered by a Catholic 'League' in 1609.

The reforms, divisions, and revolutions of the sixteenth century led to a redefining, tightening, and redrawing of geographical, ecclesiastical, and theological boundaries. At the Council of Trent the leaders of the Latin church tightened discipline and doctrine, and re-invigorated the church; a leaner, more focussed Roman Catholic Church emerged. Excluded were Lutherans, Calvinists, and Anglicans – all heirs to Catholic traditions and teachings of earlier centuries.

The Lutherans, led by Jacob Andreae (1528–90) and Martin Chemnitz (1522–86), drew up in the Formula of Concord (1577) a precise, definitive statement of belief that was signed by representatives of many German state-churches and thousands of pastors.

At the Synod of Dort (1618–19), Calvinists from the Netherlands, England, Switzerland, Scotland, the Palatinate, and other German states drew up a similar definition of their doctrine. As was the case with both the Latin church and the Lutherans, hard-line Calvinists were concerned to protect their version of Reform against dissenting voices within their own movement, such as Jakob Arminius (1560–1609) and Hugo Grotius (1583–1645), as well as against Lutherans and Roman Catholics. Leading in the formulation of Calvinist orthodoxy was Francis Gomar (1563–1641), who helped codify Reformed doctrines.

These new and rigorous versions of the three main positions were used to suppress those holding more moderate views: Catholic moderates were suppressed after Trent; Lutheran moderates after the Formula of Concord; and Arminians after Dort. But the formulae from Trent were never published in France, the Formula of Concord was not accepted by Lutherans of Hesse, Zweibrücken, Anhalt, Pomerania, Holstein, Denmark, Sweden, Nuremberg, Strasbourg, or Magdeburg; and in the Church of England Protestant doctrine was combined with traditional structures of church government such as episcopacy.

During the Middle Ages, the Latin church had adapted flexibly to varied customs and practices across Europe. Trent, the Formula of Concord, and Dort attempted to bring uniformity to large areas of the Roman Catholic, Lutheran, and Reformed or Calvinist churches respectively. To this end, lay training was provided; institutions educating the clergy were strengthened and increased in number; and the missions of all three confessions were hugely boosted.

Yet all three confessions affirmed continuity with the Church Fathers and early creeds, and with teachings and practices of the Middle Ages. The major divide remained Roman Catholic insistence upon the finality of papal authority and Protestant insistence upon the finality of Biblical rule. The Anabaptists, who repudiated all three confessions as belonging to a 'fallen' period of church history, were rejected as heretics by all three.

Legend:
- Roman Catholic
- Lutheran
- Anglican
- Calvinist/Reformed
- Calvinist influenced
- Moravian
- Orthodox
- Muslim

- Holy Roman Empire boundary
- Major Protestant university
- Major Catholic university

NORWAY

SWEDEN

Stockholm

NORTH SEA

DENMARK

Copenhagen

BALTIC SEA

LIVONIA

COURLAND

PRUSSIA

SCOTLAND

Edinburgh

Elbe R.

LITHUANIA

Dublin

IRELAND

ENGLAND

WALES

Cambridge

Oxford

London

UNITED PROVINCES

Amsterdam

Leiden

Louvain

Cologne

Rhine R.

Wittenberg

HOLY ROMAN EMPIRE

Oder R.

Warsaw

POLAND

Mainz

PALATINATE

Prague

Paris

Heidelberg

Ingolstadt

BAVARIA

Munich

Vienna

HUNGARY

Dneister R.

FRANCE

Zurich

SWISS CONFEDERATION

Geneva

VENICE

Danube R.

ATLANTIC OCEAN

Rhône R.

GENOA

NAVARRE

Ebro R.

Barcelona

PAPAL STATES

NAPLES

OTTOMAN EMPIRE
(MUSLIM MINORITY)

PORTUGAL

Salamanca

Madrid

SPAIN

SARDINIA

bon

MEDITERRANEAN SEA

SICILY

Miles
0   100   200   300

0 100 200   400
Kilometers

In the late sixteenth century, English fishing and trading posts operated for several years along the east coast of North America before permanent colonies were founded. English colonization began with the establishment of the Jamestown Colony in Virginia in 1607, mainly for commercial reasons. The rule of this colony was aristocratic and authoritarian, and the Church of England was soon established. Conflict arose between the independent farmers and artisans and the government, which wished to develop a plantation economy. In 1612 the cultivation of tobacco began and in 1619 the first African slaves arrived on a Dutch ship.

Pilgrim Fathers

In the 1620s and 1630s, English settlements motivated mainly by religious concerns were founded. The first was established in 1620 by the group of English Separatists known as the Pilgrim Fathers, who had originally left England for the Netherlands because of religious persecution. They subsequently left Europe on board the *Mayflower* to find somewhere they could freely practise their faith and set up an ideal Christian commonwealth. They arrived at Cape Cod, a little south of the territory they had actually been granted. The Pilgrims proceeded to draw up the Mayflower Compact, translating into political terms their understanding of the voluntary base of human associations that made them radical Puritans in church matters. Plymouth Colony remained relatively democratic and its congregational covenant spread to the Massachusetts Bay Colony.

Massachusetts Bay Company

Further settlements were set up in what became New Hampshire and Maine, and in 1629 and 1630 major expeditions of around 22 ships and 1,400 settlers arrived, under the auspices of the Massachusetts Bay Company. Between 1630 and 1643 some 20,000 Puritans left England, opposed to changes in the Anglican Church which they regarded as a reversion to Roman Catholic practices. Settlers in the Massachusetts Bay Colony were committed to remaining in the Church of England and working for reform from within.

Both the Pilgrims and the Massachusetts Bay Colony believed in the ideal of a Christian commonwealth governed by Christian principles, seeking to achieve the earthly prototype of the heavenly city. The first governor of the Massachusetts Bay Colony, John Winthrop (1588–1649), famously stated, 'We must consider that we shall be as a city upon a hill, the eyes of all people are upon us.' In order to become a *member* of the church or a *citizen* in the colony, an individual had to testify to having experienced true Christian conversion; all others were considered mere 'attendees' of the church and 'inhabitants' of the colony. The leaders considered themselves in a covenant with God and carried out their secular duties as a religious calling. Massachusetts, with its early villages at Salem, Boston, Dorchester, Watertown, established a state church and a representative assembly, or 'General Court', that replaced an earlier open assembly of free citizens. By 1636 Harvard College had been established.

Conflicts arose early between establishment orthodoxy and dissenters like Anne Hutchinson and Roger Williams, who moved to frontier settlements such as Providence and Hartford, where they could better explore religious freedom, political democracy, and economic opportunity. In 1636 Roger Williams (c. 1603–83) founded

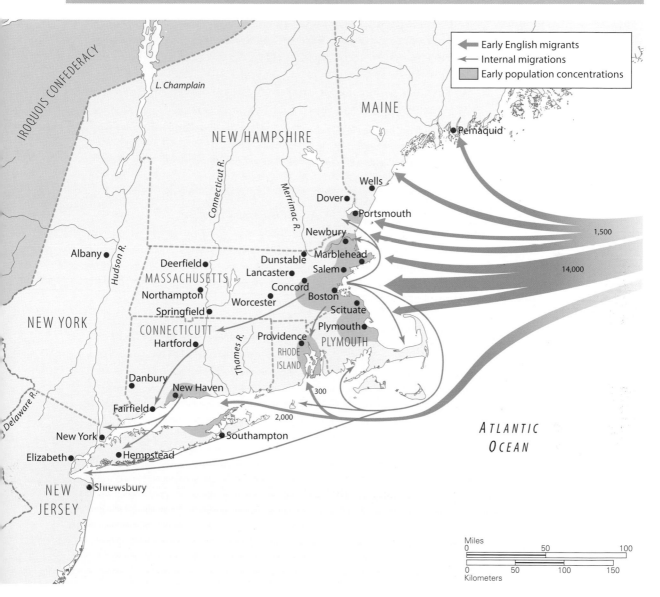

Providence Plantation on Rhode Island, a colony characterized by religious diversity. The Baptists who settled there committed to another characteristic of future American politics: the separation of church and state.

Charles V had always held precarious control over the Holy Roman Empire, a patchwork of more than 300 principalities, church states, and free cities, all jealously guarding their liberties against any attempts by the Emperor to increase his authority. He had not been able even to raise effective support from Catholic states to help suppress the Lutherans, since Catholic princes feared success might give him increased power over them too.

The size of his empire presented Charles with many problems, principally military threats from France and the Ottoman Turks. As a result, Charles had been forced to ignore the Protestants while he dealt with urgent matters on his borders. Not until 1546 was he able to attack the defensive alliance of Lutheran princes known as the Schmalkaldic League. Although he won a decisive military victory, the factors summarized above prevented him from imposing firm imperial control and his Catholic faith in Germany; Lutheranism and the political privileges of the German princes were both too deeply entrenched.

Cuius regio, eius religio

In 1555 Charles reluctantly agreed to the Peace of Augsburg, a compromise that gave each German prince the right to choose his realm's religion – provided it was either Catholic or Lutheran. The prince could decide the faith of his subjects on the basis '*cuius regio, eius religio*' ('whose the rule, his the religion'; a phrase coined in the late sixteenth century, but the operating principle of the Peace of Westphalia in 1648), although Calvinists, Anabaptists, Socinians, and other non-Lutheran Protestants were still not to be tolerated.

Instead of settling Germany's religious problems, the Peace of Augsburg actually exacerbated them, leading to thousands of refugees – especially the Reformed and Anabaptists – fleeing Germany and spreading their religious beliefs to the Netherlands, France, and England. Charles V, worn out by more than thirty years' struggle to maintain his empire and religious unity, gave up his throne. The family lands in Austria and the Imperial title now went to his brother Ferdinand.

Religious tensions

Despite the Peace of Augsburg, Calvinism and Reformed Protestantism continued to spread across Germany, further raising religious tensions. Calvinists gained from the Lutherans major states such as the Palatinate, Ansbach, and Hesse, while states such as Brandenburg became a mix of Lutheran and Reformed, instead of solely Lutheran as before. Strong bodies of Reform also existed in Hungary; the Magyars preferred Calvinism to the early Lutheranism, which they associated with German domination of Hungary.

Powered by the Counter-Reformation, the Roman Catholic Church had reclaimed lands lost earlier to Protestantism. Some territories had always remained loyal to Rome, but the concentrated efforts of the Jesuits in particular now succeeded in bringing others back to the Latin Church.

Nevertheless the largest Reformation group in Germany continued to be Lutheran. Having emerged from the Schmalkaldic War, the Interims, and the War of Liberation, Lutheranism was now stabilized in its northern strongholds.

Miles
0   100   200

0   100   200   300
Kilometers

NORTH SEA

BALTIC SEA

DENMARK

• Königsberg
PRUSSIA

HULSTEIN

BREMEN *MECKLENBURG* *POMERANIA*

Hamburg •
Elbe R.

OLDENBURG

BRUNSWICK *BRANDENBURG*
Oder R.

• Berlin

UNITED PROVINCES
Amsterdam •
Münster •
MAGDEBURG

POLAND

MÜNSTER

Rhine R.

GERMANY
• Wittenberg

Cologne •
• Leipzig

HESSE
SAXONY
• Dresden
SILESIA

SPANISH NETHERLANDS

HANAU
NASSAU

Mainz • • Frankfurt
Prague •
BOHEMIA

LUXEMBOURG
PALATINATE

Trier •
UPPER PALATINATE
MORAVIA

LORRAINE

• Nuremberg

WÜRTTEMBERG

Strasbourg •
Augsburg •
BAVARIA
AUSTRIA
HUNGARY

Vienna •

Basel •
• Munich
Danube R.

Salzburg •
STYRIA

• Zurich
SALZBURG

SWISS CONFEDERATION
TYROL
CARINTHIA

OTTOMAN
EMPIRE
(MUSLIM MINORITY)

FRANCE
(CALVINIST/HUGUENOT MINORITY)

Geneva •
CARNIOLA

Milan •

VENICE

Genoa •
• Venice

SAVOY

ADRIATIC SEA

Legend:
— Holy Roman Empire boundary
Catholic
Lutheran
Anglican
Calvinist/Reformed
Zwinglian
Moravian minority
Recovered by Catholics
Orthodox
Muslim

The Thirty Years' War

In central Europe, hostilities bubbling beneath the surface broke out again in 1618. The war started in Bohemia, long destabilized by the forces of Muslim invaders, the Reformation and Counter-Reformation, the Hungarian, Bohemian, and Transylvanian aristocracies, and Habsburg territorial claims. In 1617, the Habsburg heir, Ferdinand of Styria (1578–1637), was elected king of Protestant Bohemia. Ferdinand, a Jesuit-educated Catholic, was already notorious for his persecution of Lutherans in Austria. He sent two Catholic deputies to Bohemia, to which the Protestants reacted with fury, throwing them out of a palace window (the 'defenestration of Prague'). When the Bohemian Protestants called for military support, the Protestant Union responded and initially defeated the imperial forces.

The Thirty Years' War consisted of a series of wars – Bohemian, Danish, Swedish, and Swedish-French – named for the place of major conflict or leading powers involved, but considered as a single unit because of the final comprehensive peace settlement – the Treaties of Westphalia (1648). The first phase of the war (1618–29) was primarily religious; the second (1630–48) largely a struggle over the power of the Habsburg dynasty and the influence of Sweden and France within the Holy Roman Empire.

In 1620 the Bohemian army, led by Frederick V, Elector Palatine from the Rhineland, who had been offered the crown of Bohemia by the rebellious Estates, was routed by a Catholic coalition led by Baron Tilly at the Battle of the White Mountain. Over the next two years, Bavarian and Spanish armies conquered the Palatinate and reclaimed it for Catholicism.

The widespread use of mercenary armies helped make this war particularly devastating for inhabitants of the Holy Roman Empire, as the armies lived off the land and pillaged the countryside. Mercenary leaders such as Ernst von Mansfeld (1580–1626) and Albrecht von Wallenstein (1583–1634) were happy to fight for either side if sufficiently rewarded. Although labelled a religious war, political factors and the naked desire for personal gain also played a major role.

In 1625 the Lutheran Christian IV of Denmark (1588–1648) entered the war in an attempt to prevent total Catholic victory. But, unable to find German allies, Christian was defeated by the Bavarians under Tilly at Lutter (1626). Wallenstein now occupied much of Denmark as well as Brandenburg for the Emperor, while his troops also took Magdeburg and the major Lutheran city of Augsburg, forcing both cities to reconvert to Catholicism.

At this point the Emperor was in a position to rescind the Peace of Augsburg and reimpose Catholicism in the Empire. The Edict of Restitution (1629) outlawed Reform and Calvinism and forced the Lutherans to restore church properties they had secularized.

However the Swedish king, Gustavus Adolphus (1594–1632), now arrived with an army in Pomerania, committed to relieving his fellow Lutherans. Although he met difficulties winning the support of the German Lutheran princes, he received a subsidy from Cardinal Richelieu, the French king's chief minister, who had a predatory eye on imperial territory in the Rhineland. Adolphus, an outstanding military leader, won the most decisive military victory of the war at Breitenfeld (1631), thereby saving the Protestant cause. The following year he met Wallenstein at the Battle of Lutzen: the imperial forces were defeated but Gustavus Adolphus himself was killed. Wallenstein was assassinated in 1634.

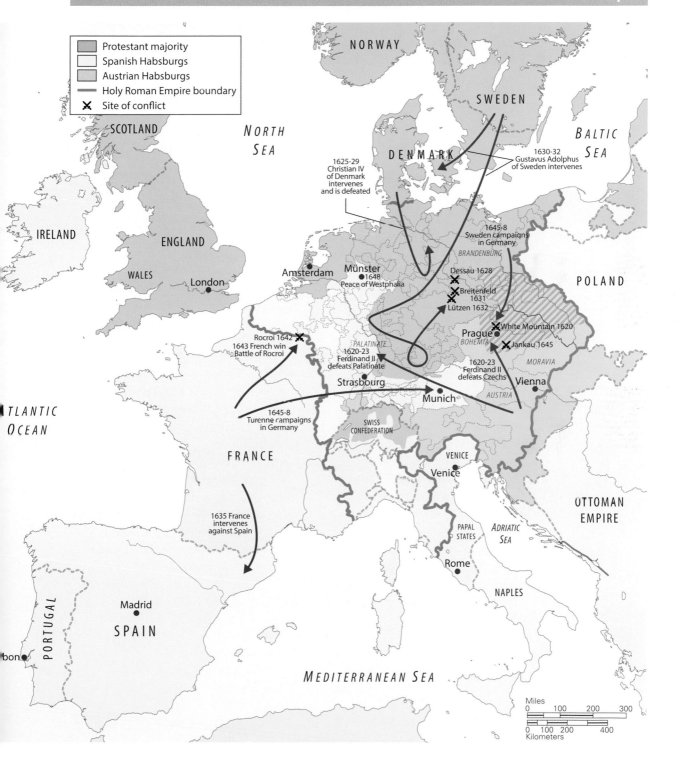

Protestant majority
Spanish Habsburgs
Austrian Habsburgs
Holy Roman Empire boundary
Site of conflict

NORWAY

SWEDEN

SCOTLAND

NORTH SEA

BALTIC SEA

DENMARK

IRELAND

ENGLAND

WALES

London

1625-29
Christian IV
of Denmark
intervenes
and is defeated

1630-32
Gustavus Adolphus
of Sweden intervenes

BRANDENBURG

1645-8
Sweden campaigns
in Germany

POLAND

Amsterdam

Münster
1648
Peace of Westphalia

Dessau 1628
Breitenfeld
1631
Lützen 1632

White Mountain 1620
Prague
BOHEMIA
Jankau 1645

MORAVIA

Rocroi 1642
1643 French win
Battle of Rocroi

PALATINATE
1620-23
Ferdinand II
defeats Palatinate

1620-23
Ferdinand II
defeats Czechs

Vienna

Strasbourg

Munich

AUSTRIA

ATLANTIC OCEAN

1645-8
Turenne campaigns
in Germany

SWISS
CONFEDERATION

FRANCE

VENICE
Venice

OTTOMAN
EMPIRE

1635 France
intervenes
against Spain

PAPAL
STATES

ADRIATIC
SEA

Rome

Madrid

NAPLES

PORTUGAL

SPAIN

bon

MEDITERRANEAN SEA

Miles
0   100   200   300

0   100 200   400
Kilometers

After the War

Although the most successful generals had now died, the Thirty Years' War dragged on, the tide of battle ebbing and flowing inconclusively. It became clear after the Battle of Nordlingen (1634) that the Catholics could not hold northern Germany, nor the Protestants southern. With French forces now involved on the Protestant side with the Swedes, the war continued for thirteen more years. After lengthy negotiations, compromise prevailed and finally the Peace of Westphalia was signed (October 1648).

By the settlements of Westphalia, France received Metz, Verdun, Toul, and lands in Alsace and Lorraine, while Sweden gained a beachhead in western Pomerania. Brandenburg acquired eastern Pomerania, Magdeburg, and several bishoprics; Saxony acquired Lusatia; Bavaria gained territory in the Palatinate and became one of the imperial electors, supplanting the Elector Palatine. Switzerland and the United Provinces in the Low Countries were both accorded independence.

Territorial adjustments

Although ostensibly a war of religion, the bloodletting did not significantly alter the confessional picture of central Europe. The Peace of Westphalia reaffirmed the Peace of Augsburg, except that the Reformed Churches were now awarded the same legal recognition as Roman Catholics and Lutherans, the choice of permitted faith depending upon the government of the respective territory. With the exception of lands of the Austrian Habsburgs, where Counter Reformation gains were allowed to stand, areas that were Protestant or Catholic in January 1624 (i.e. before most of the re-Catholicization of ecclesiastical territory in northern Germany but after the conquest of the Palatinate) would remain so.

Catastrophe

The biggest losers in the war were the German people. For thirty years armies had lived off the land, looting, raping, and destroying. Plague and famine followed the mercenary armies, and cannibalism was reported in several starvation areas. The Thirty Years' War reduced Germany to crude barbarism and brought to an end numerous smaller political units. The Empire suffered severe population loss. It has been estimated there were eight million fewer inhabitants in Germany at the end of the war than at the beginning; the conflict reduced the population by at least 25 per cent and possibly by 35 or 40 per cent.

Quietism

Religious developments reflected the misery of the people who had suffered so much from the armies, pestilence, and starvation. There was an upsurge of personal mysticism, of which Jakob Boehme (1575–1624) is representative. He repudiated the material world, and accentuated the hope of heaven; his writings reflect ecstasy in the divine presence in the soul.

Population loss
- 0 – 33%
- 34 – 66%
- more than 66%

✗ Significant battle
— Holy Roman Empire boundary

DENMARK

BALTIC SEA

NORTH SEA

HOLSTEIN

BREMEN

MECKLENBURG

POMERANIA

Wolfgast 1628 ✗
Goldberg 1635 ✗
✗ Wittstock 1636
✗ Dömitz 1635

Bremen •

Elbe R.

BRANDENBURG

Oder R.

• Berlin

POLAND

UNITED PROVINCES

• Amsterdam

Lutter 1626 ✗

MAGDEBURG

Aschersleben 1645 ✗

SPANISH NETHERLANDS

✗ Kempen 1642

WESTPHALIA

Weser R.

✗ Dessau 1626

✗ Breitenfeld 1631

LUSATIA

✗ Glogau 1642

Steinau 1633 ✗

• Antwerp

Lützen 1632 ✗

SAXONY

SILESIA

Kosel 1627 ✗

Rhine R.

✗ White Mountain 1620

• Frankfurt

Main R.

Mainz •

PALATINATE

Mergentheim 1645 ✗

✗ Nuremberg 1632

Prague •

Jankau 1645 ✗

BOHEMIA

Krakow •

Weisloch 1622 ✗
✗ Wimpfen 1622

MORAVIA

✗ Netolitz 1619

LORRAINE

Strasbourg •

Zumarshausen 1648 ✗

✗ Nördlingen 1634,35

✗ Rain 1632

HUNGARY

FRANCE

Wittenweier 1638 ✗

Wattweiler 1639 ✗

✗ Tuttlingen 1643

BAVARIA

✗ Eferding 1626

Vienna •

AUSTRIA

Rheinfelden 1638 ✗

Danube R.

Sennheim 1638 ✗

SWISS CONFEDERATION

OTTOMAN EMPIRE

SAVOY

VENICE

• Venice

• Milan

Miles
0   50   100   150

0   100   200
Kilometers

ADRIATIC SEA

Europe 1648

The Treaty of Westphalia marked the end of the last major religious war in Europe. This settlement, the first time a diplomatic congress brought together all the interested parties to address and determine a dispute, served as a model for resolving conflict among warring European nations.

Europe would never be the same. Cardinal Richelieu had made Louis XIV supreme in France, and France the leader of Europe. As a victor in the war, France acquired Alsace-Lorraine and other smaller territories.

Sweden, like France, emerged victorious, controlling the Baltic Sea, and becoming the most powerful nation in northern Europe.

Spain and the Holy Roman Empire now recognized the independence of Switzerland.

By the Treaty of Münster (1648), Spain also recognized the independence of the United Provinces as the Dutch Republic, ending eighty years of conflict between the Dutch and the Spanish. Meanwhile Spain and the Spanish Habsburgs lost colonies and territorial possession.

The German princes had won sovereignty, with each state gaining the power to make its own laws instead of obeying the Emperor. Each prince could also now choose the Reformed Church or Calvinism as well as Lutheranism or Roman Catholicism as the confession of his realm. But Germany remained divided into hundreds of individual, sovereign states, governed by their respective princes. 1648 effectively marked an end to the influence of the Holy Roman Empire, since the princes were now sovereign in their territories.

For Catholicism, Westphalia marked the end of the enforced Counter-Reformation. Whereas up to 1648 religion was a significant determining factor of internal and external politics, this was much less so after the Thirty Years' War.

Legend:
- Catholic
- Catholic influenced
- Lutheran
- Anglican
- Calvinist/Reformed
- Calvinist influenced
- Moravian minority
- Orthodox
- Muslim
- —— Holy Roman Empire boundary
- - - - Extent of Ottoman Empire

NORWAY
Christiania (Oslo)
Stockholm
SWEDEN
BALTIC SEA
LIVONIA
COURLAND
Copenhagen
DENMARK
PRUSSIA
RUSSIA
UNITED PROVINCES
Elbe R.
Berlin
Hanover
BRANDENBURG
Vistula R.
LITHUANIA
HOLY ROMAN EMPIRE
SAXONY
Dresden
SILESIA
Oder R.
Warsaw
POLAND
Rhine R.
PALATINATE
Nuremberg
Prague
BOHEMIA
MORAVIA
Kiev
Dnieper R.
WÜRTTEMBERG
BAVARIA
AUSTRIA
Vienna
HUNGARY
Dneister R.
Strasbourg
Danube R.
TRANSYLVANIA
MOLDAVIA
Basel
SWISS CONFEDERATION
Geneva
VENICE
Venice
WALLACHIA
Genoa
BOSNIA
Florence
TUSCANY
SERBIA
OTTOMAN EMPIRE (MUSLIM MINORITY)
CORSICA
PAPAL STATES
Rome
NAPLES
Naples
SARDINIA
GREECE
OTTOMAN EMPIRE
MEDITERRANEAN SEA
SICILY
CRETE
CYPRUS

Several European nations undertook settlements in North America. The Spanish made extensive settlements as they pushed north from the empire of New Spain into what are now Florida and Louisiana; and on the south-west coast, Texas, New Mexico, Arizona, and California.

While the Catholic Reformation was inspiring worldwide missionary effort, Protestant countries such as England and the Netherlands were also exploring and colonizing, though not so active in evangelizing the peoples they contacted.

Dutch traders founded New Amsterdam in 1626, after more than ten years' profitable fur trading along the Hudson River. In 1664 this town was captured by English forces, who renamed it New York.

From 1638, the Swedes made settlements along the Delaware River, but the Dutch captured Fort Christiana and controlled New Sweden from 1655, until the English captured it.

Maryland

In 1634 English Roman Catholics, including two Jesuit priests, arrived in Maryland to settle an area granted to Lord Calvert by Charles I. In 1649 the Maryland legislature passed an act of religious toleration that was in advance of the times. However, during the English Civil War, Protestants seized the Maryland colony and repealed the Toleration Act. After the Restoration, the Church of England was made the established church here.

Later in the seventeenth century, William Penn founded the Quaker colony of Pennsylvania, which also attracted Mennonites and Lutherans.

To the south of Virginia, in the Carolinas and Georgia, a mixed religious tradition prevailed. These colonies, run by gentlemen plantation-owners who worked slaves, were officially Anglican. Mainly Puritan small-holders and artisans moved west into the foothills of the Appalachian Mountains.

Protestant missions

Protestant colonists had limited success sharing their faith with Native Americans. One of the earliest efforts was by John Eliot (1604–90), an Anglican clergyman who went to New England in 1631 and started evangelizing Native Americans in 1646. When it seemed converts could not live as Christians within their tribe, Eliot established 'Praying Towns', quite similar to the Jesuit Reductions of South America. By 1671 Eliot had established fourteen such self-governing communities, composed of around 3,600 members. He also started to train Native American clergy and translated the Bible into their language. Another missionary to the Native Americans, Thomas Mayhew Jr. (1618–57), began work in Martha's Vineyard in 1647. It's estimated that by 1675, when King Philip's War disrupted these activities, approximately 20 per cent of the Native American population of New England was at least nominally Christian.

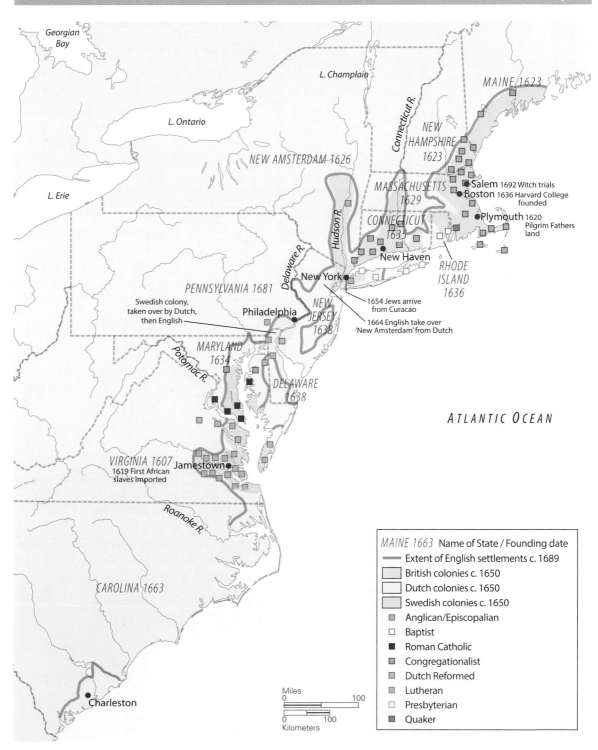

Georgian Bay

L. Champlain

L. Ontario

L. Erie

MAINE 1623

Connecticut R.

NEW HAMPSHIRE 1623

NEW AMSTERDAM 1626

MASSACHUSETTS 1629

Salem 1692 Witch trials
Boston 1636 Harvard College founded
Plymouth 1620 Pilgrim Fathers land

CONNECTICUT 1635

Hudson R.

New Haven

RHODE ISLAND 1636

Delaware R.

New York

1654 Jews arrive from Curacao

PENNSYLVANIA 1681

Swedish colony, taken over by Dutch, then English

Philadelphia

NEW JERSEY 1638

1664 English take over 'New Amsterdam' from Dutch

MARYLAND 1634

Potomac R.

DELAWARE 1638

ATLANTIC OCEAN

VIRGINIA 1607 Jamestown
1619 First African slaves imported

Roanoke R.

CAROLINA 1663

Charleston

Miles
0   100
0   100
Kilometers

MAINE 1663 Name of State / Founding date
Extent of English settlements c. 1689
British colonies c. 1650
Dutch colonies c. 1650
Swedish colonies c. 1650
Anglican/Episcopalian
Baptist
Roman Catholic
Congregationalist
Dutch Reformed
Lutheran
Presbyterian
Quaker

When Queen Elizabeth I died in 1603, it seemed she had achieved her objective of avoiding religious war in England. She had prevented the Puritans from altering her religious settlement, while keeping most of them within the Church of England.

James Stuart, King of Scotland 1567–1625, who succeeded to the English throne in 1603 as James I, also managed to avoid agreeing to the Puritans' demands without alienating them. He accepted moderate Puritans' demand at the Hampton Court Conference for one agreed English translation of the Bible, which resulted in the King James Version – often now referred to as the Authorized Version – published in 1611. During James's reign, the Elizabethan Settlement remained intact and the Church of England broad enough to contain all but radical Separatists or committed Roman Catholics.

Charles I

This stability ended during the reign of his son, Charles I, who antagonized those who wished to be loyal subjects but were disturbed by his religious policy. The Puritans became particularly concerned when he promoted as church leaders those they considered 'Arminians', associated with High Church practice.

Charles was completely unsympathetic to Calvinism and appointed as Archbishop of Canterbury the Arminian William Laud (r. 1633–45), who began stringently to enforce rules of worship and to coerce and dismiss ministers who refused to conform. Many Puritans departed for North America, while others remained and opposed Charles. The Puritans enjoyed strong support among the gentry in Parliament; when

Charles tried to stop Parliament dealing with matters he considered royal business, they protested strongly.

When Laud attempted to impose ecclesiastical uniformity on Scotland, the Scots drew up a National Covenant denouncing the new prayer book, and in 1638 abolished the episcopacy. A Scottish army invaded England, forcing the king to call Parliament to raise money to wage war. The first Parliament failed to comply, so in 1640 he called the 'Long Parliament',

King Charles I.

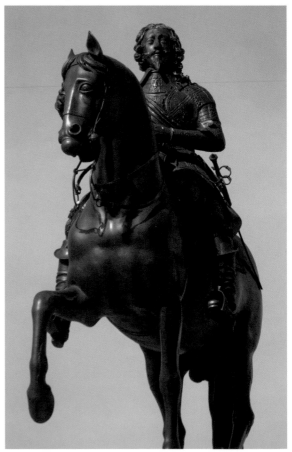

SCOTLAND

NORTH
SEA

Area held by Parliament in 1643
Area held by Charles I in 1643
✗ Royalist victory
✗ Parliament victory
✗ Indecisive

IRISH
SEA

IRELAND

●York

Humber R.

1643
Adwalton Moor

E N G L A N D

To Amsterdam
1609 John Smyth founds
first English Baptist church

Trent R.

Norwich●
EAST
ANGLIA

Severn R.

1642 Edgehill,
'Kineton Fight'

Avon R.

WALES

Oxford

1612 Thomas Helwys
founds first Baptist church
in England

Bristol●

●London

1643
Newbury

1642
Turnham Green

Thames R.

ATLANTIC
OCEAN

WEST COUNTRY

Exeter●

ENGLISH CHANNEL

FRANCE

Miles
0 10   30   50

0 10   30   50
Kilometers

with whom he struggled constantly. The Catholic-led Irish Rebellion broke out in 1641, resulting in the deaths of thousands of Protestant settlers in Ulster.

War begins

In August 1642, Charles I left London to raise his standard at Nottingham. The ensuing English Civil War was a struggle between king and Parliament over constitutional issues, but also a war about religion. Neither side wanted this conflict and both suffered severely. The Puritans eventually succeeded in defeating the king, but then faced new problems, including divisions among themselves and the difficulty of achieving their goal of a godly commonwealth.

Charles I lost the Civil War. Oliver Cromwell (1599–1658), a gifted general, became political leader of the Parliamentary army, and his force of committed Puritans, the 'New Model Army', beat a much more experienced army led by battle-hardened generals. The decisive battle occurred at Naseby (1645), where Cromwell's disciplined soldiers defeated the king's forces.

The Parliamentary party was prepared for a settlement that provided for greater religious liberty, parliamentary reform, and the return to power of Charles I. However the king escaped, made an alliance with the Scots, and re-started the war. After Charles had been defeated a second time, Cromwell decided he had to pay with his life. Charles I was executed in January 1649.

The defeat of the monarchy revealed religious divisions among the victorious Puritans, but as Lord Protector Cromwell held his divided country together while he lived. Cromwell faced a proliferation of sects such as the millenarian Fifth Monarchists, who were prepared to use violence to achieve their ends. Others, such as the Levellers and Diggers, had radical political and socio-economic agendas.

Westminster Confession

The Westminster Assembly (1643–53), called to implement an agreed religious settlement, comprised Calvinists from England and Scotland, who divided over questions of church government. The majority were committed to a Presbyterian system, but some argued for a modified episcopacy, while the 'Independents' rejected both forms of church government. Out of their deliberations came one of the great Reformed creeds, the Westminster Confession.

Restoration

When Cromwell died, his son Richard succeeded as Lord Protector, but lasted less than a year. Charles I's son, Charles II (r. 1660–85), returned to rule a kingdom whose religious divisions were obvious. His Restoration Settlement restored the Church of England as the Established Church and imposed stringent regulations on Puritans in the so-called Clarendon Code (1661–65), which eventually drove most of them out of the Anglican Church. Many Puritans became Separatists, and the Church of England lost numerous gifted and zealous ministers.

The Civil War – one of the bloodiest conflicts in English history – was a disaster during which one in fourteen adult males was killed. It heralded the way for the modern age, in which religion was relegated to a private matter. Within three decades of the Restoration Settlement, England adopted a form of religious toleration that embraced all but Roman Catholics and anti-trinitarians.

Engraving of King Charles II.

ATLANTIC
OCEAN

Aberdeen September 1644 ✗

SCOTLAND

NORTH
SEA

Edinburgh

IRELAND

IRISH
SEA

ENGLAND

York ✗
Marston Moor
September 1644

Preston ✗
August 1648

Trent R.

Norwich ●

EAST
ANGLIA

c. 1647
George Fox
founds Friends,
'Quakers'

Naseby ✗
June 1645

WALES

Stow-on-the-Wold ✗
March 1646

Oxford ●

1649
Charles I beheaded

Severn R.

Newbury ✗
October 1644

London

Bristol ●

Cheriton ✗
March 1644

Thames R.

Langport ✗
July 1645

Exeter ●

WEST COUNTRY

Plymouth ●

ENGLISH CHANNEL

FRANCE

Miles
0 10   30   50

0 10   30   50
Kilometers

Legend:
- Scottish Royalist area of influence
- Scottish Presbyterian area of influence
- Area held by Parliament November 1644
- Territory taken from Royalists by November 1645
- Area held by Royalists November 1645
- ✗ Royalist victory
- ✗ Parliament victory

As Lord Protector, Cromwell hoped to construct a Protestant League in Northern Europe. He settled disputes between Denmark and Sweden, concluded an alliance with Sweden, formed strong links with Holland, negotiated peace between the Protestant nations, cleared the English Channel of pirates, and expanded foreign trade.

Between 1649 and 1652, Cromwell subdued a Royalist-backed revolt in Ireland, where his forces committed brutal massacres at the towns of Drogheda and Wexford.

A key feature of Cromwell's foreign policy was his use of sea power: in 1653 he had 180 ships at his disposal, more than France, Spain, or the Netherlands.

In 1654 Cromwell secretly promoted a 'Western Design', to attack Spanish colonies in the West Indies. He demanded that English subjects in Spanish territories should have freedom of worship and that English traders should not be molested. To enforce this, in 1655 he sent a poorly equipped force to San Domingo and Jamaica, and succeeded in taking the latter territory. Cromwell had hoped Puritans from New England might settle there; instead, it became a place to which the English shipped criminals and rebels. Cromwell also regained for England Virginia and the Barbados Islands.

In April 1655, Cromwell's navy attacked a pirate stronghold in Tunis, North Africa, and forced the sultan to release English prisoners and slaves.

In May 1655, the Catholic Duke of Savoy started viciously to persecute the Protestant Waldensians in his territory. Cromwell sent an agent to investigate, headed a subscription list raising funds for the relief of the victims, and demanded the duke cease his oppression.

Jewish return

The Jews had been expelled from England in 1290. Cromwell favoured freedom of religion and wished to see the fulfilment of a prophecy that the Jews would find salvation in Christ, ushering in the Last Days. Hence he informally invited the Jews to return, provided they did not take their worship into the public square, and hosted their leader, Menasseh Ben Israel (1604–57), at a reception in Whitehall.

In June 1658, an English force defeated the Spanish at Mardyk, Gravelines, and Dunkirk. As payment for fighting alongside the French, Cromwell gained for England the port of Dunkirk, which Charles II later promptly sold back to France.

Oliver Cromwell (1599–1658).

Miles
0   100   200   300

0   100   200   400
Kilometers

NORTH SEA

NORWAY

SWEDEN

SCOTLAND

1650
Subdues and
garrisons Scotland

●Edinburgh

DENMARK

1649–50
Re-conquers
Ireland

●Dublin

IRELAND

ENGLAND

WALES

1653
Defeats Dutch
navy
✕

London●

ENGLISH CHANNEL

●Dunkirk
1658 Takes Dunkirk
from Spain

Rhine R.

Elbe R.

1654
Takes Jamaica
from Spain

●Paris

Danube R.

1657
Destroys Spanish
fleet off Tenerife

FRANCE

SWISS
CONFEDERATION

Cromwell protests Duke of Savoy's
persecution of Waldensians

SAVOY

ATLANTIC
OCEAN

●Bordeaux

Rhône R.

Ebro R.

PORTUGAL

Madrid●

Tagus R.

SPAIN

MEDITERRANEAN SEA

1660
English fleet
bombards Tunis

Lisbon●

Cartagena●

1652 Destroys
Prince Rupert's
fleet

1655 Defeats
Algerian pirates

●Tunis

1656
Plunders silver and
gold from Spanish fleet

●Cadiz

Algiers●

Mission to Japan

The Jesuit Francis Xavier arrived in Japan in 1549, just six years after the first Portuguese traders. In Goa he had met a Japanese called Yajiro, who told him of his native country. Xavier arrived in Japan accompanied by two fellow Jesuits and Yajiro, who had now converted to Christianity. At first Xavier achieved little; yet he admired the Japanese, claiming 'these Japanese are more ready to be implanted with our holy faith than all the nations of the world'. He stayed more than two years and left behind the earliest Japanese converts.

After Xavier's death, other Jesuits carried on his work, achieving considerable success. By 1600, the Japanese church numbered more than 300,000 members. Initially the situation favoured the missionaries: political power rested with some 250 *daimyos* (local feudal chiefs) and Buddhism was in decline. The Jesuits gained the support of some local *daimyos*, and established a seminary to train Japanese priests.

When central authority was re-established, the monarch became suspicious of Christians, who he thought were subversive and allied with local chiefs. In 1593, Spanish Franciscans arrived in Japan, and rivalry between the Christian powers led the ruler, Toyotomi Hideyoski, to turn against believers. In 1597 he crucified twenty Japanese priests and six Spaniards in Nagasaki, and expelled both the Jesuits and Franciscans. His successor, Tokugawa Ieyasu, initially allied with several Christian *daimyos* and tolerated Christians. But when the Dutch replaced the Portuguese as Japan's chief trading partner, they and the English warned the Japanese ruler against Spanish imperialism.

Persecution

Finally the Japanese Shogun lost patience and in 1614 issued an edict: 'The Kirishitan [Christian] band have come to Japan . . . to disseminate an evil law, to overthrow true doctrine, so that they may change the government of the country and obtain possession of the land. This is the germ of great disaster, and must be crushed.'

This resulted in the brutal persecution of Christians, especially after a peasant uprising in which Christians played a leading role was suppressed in 1637–38. Christians were cruelly treated to persuade them to apostatize. Tortured to the point of death, punishment was halted until they recovered sufficiently, when they were tortured again. This cycle was repeated until they relinquished their faith. Many Christians were also executed – Japanese Christians crucified and Europeans burned at the stake. It has been estimated as many as 6,000 Christians died as a result of this persecution.

In 1640 the Japanese government set up an Office of Inquisition for Christian Affairs to root out Christians. In an attempt to reveal secret Christians, they introduced the ceremony of 'picture-stamping', when people were ordered to trample on pictures of Jesus and the Virgin Mary. The Japanese church was all but eradicated; only a tiny remnant survived.

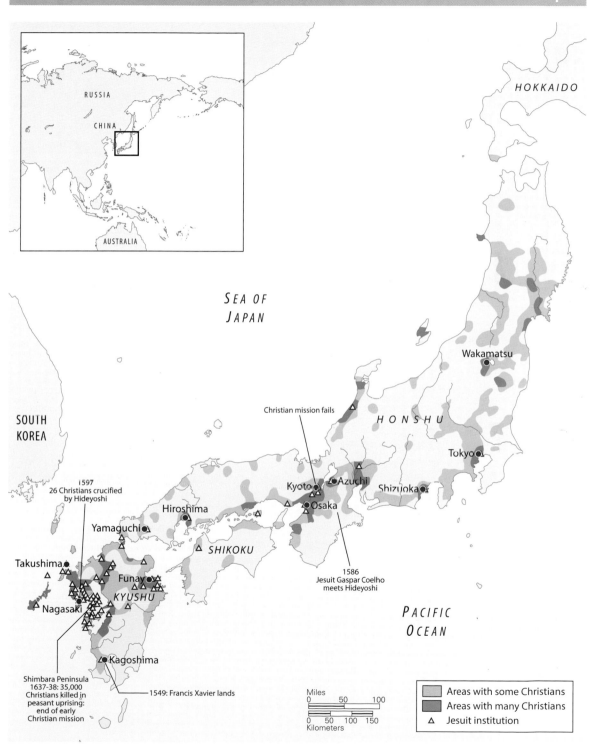

RUSSIA

CHINA

AUSTRALIA

HOKKAIDO

SEA OF
JAPAN

Wakamatsu

Christian mission fails

HONSHU

SOUTH
KOREA

Tokyo

1597
26 Christians crucified
by Hideyoshi

Kyoto

Azuchi

Shizuoka

Hiroshima

Osaka

Yamaguchi

1586
Jesuit Gaspar Coelho
meets Hideyoshi

Takushima

SHIKOKU

Funay

KYUSHU

Nagasaki

PACIFIC
OCEAN

Kagoshima

Shimbara Peninsula
1637-38: 35,000
Christians killed in
peasant uprising:
end of early
Christian mission

1549: Francis Xavier lands

Miles
0   50   100

0   50   100   150
Kilometers

Areas with some Christians
Areas with many Christians
△ Jesuit institution

Further reading

The Late Middle Ages

Eamon Duffy, *Saints and Sinners: A History of the Popes*, 3rd ed. (New Haven: Yale University Press, 2006).

Alister E. McGrath, *The Intellectual Origins of the European Reformation*, 2nd ed. (Cambridge, MA: Blackwell, 2003).

Heiko A. Oberman, *The Reformation: Roots and Ramifications* (Grand Rapids: Eerdmans, 1994).

Matthew Spinka, *John Hus at the Council of Constance* (New York: Columbia University Press, 1965).

Cornelius Augustijn, *Erasmus: His Life, Works, and Influence*, trans. G. C. Grayson (Toronto: University of Toronto Press, 1996).

William J. Bouwsma, *The Waning of the Renaissance, 1550–1640* (New Haven: Yale University Press, 2002).

The Reformation

Euan Cameron, *The European Reformation* (New York: Oxford University Press, 1991).

Carter Lindberg, *The European Reformations*, 2nd ed. (Oxford: Wiley-Blackwell, 2009).

Diarmaid MacCulloch, *The Reformation: A History* (New York: Viking Press, 2004).

Owen Chadwick, *The Early Reformation on the Continent*, Oxford History of the Christian Church (New York: Oxford University Press, 2002).

Felicity Heal, *Reformation in Britain and Ireland*, Oxford History of the Christian Church (New York: Oxford University Press, 2005).

Hans J. Hillerbrand, *The Division of Christendom: Christianity in the Sixteenth Century* (Louisville, KY: Westminster John Knox, 2007).

Nicholas Hope, *German and Scandinavian Protestantism 1700–1918*, Oxford History of the Christian Church (New York: Oxford University Press, 1999).

R. Po-Chia Hsia, ed., *Reform and Expansion, 1500–1600*, The Cambridge History of Christianity, Vol. 6 (Cambridge: Cambridge University Press, 2007).

R.W. Scribner & C. Scott Dixon, *The German Reformation*, 2nd ed. (Palgrave Macmillan, 2003).

George H. Williams, *Radical Reformation*, 3rd ed. (Truman State University Press, 2000).

Steven Ozment, *The Reformation in the Cities: The Appeal of Protestantism to Sixteenth-Century Germany and Switzerland* (New Haven: Yale University Press, 1975).

Reformation theology

Alister E. McGrath, *Reformation Thought: An Introduction*, 4th ed. (Oxford: Wiley-Blackwell, 2012).

David Bagchi & David Steinmetz, eds., *The Cambridge Companion to Reformation Theology* (Cambridge: Cambridge University Press, 2004).

Martin Luther

Martin Brecht, *Martin Luther: His Road to Reformation, 1483–1521*; *Martin Luther: Shaping and Defining the Reformation, 1521–1532*; and *Martin Luther: the Preservation of the Church, 1532–1546* (Minneapolis: Fortress Press, 1990–1994).

Hans-Martin Barth, *The Theology of Martin Luther: A Critical Assessment* (Minneapolis, MN: Fortress Press, 2012).

Eric W. Gritsch, *A History of Lutheranism*, 2nd ed. (Minneapolis, MN: Fortress Press, 2010).

James M. Kittelson, *Luther the Reformer: The Story of the Man and His Career* (reprint: Minneapolis: Fortress, 1993).

David C. Steinmetz, *Reformers in the Wings: From Geiler von Kaysersberg to Theodore Beza*, 2nd ed. (New York: Oxford University Press, 2000).

John Calvin

Alister McGrath, *A Life of John Calvin: A Study in the Shaping of Western Culture* (Cambridge, MA: Blackwell, 1990).

Irene Backus and Philip Benedict, eds., *Calvin and His Influence, 1509–2009* (New York: Oxford University Press, 2011).

Bernard Cottret, *Calvin: A Biography*, trans. M. Wallace MacDonald (Grand Rapids: Eerdmans, 2000).

Andrew Pettegree, Alastair Duke, & Gillian Lewis, ed., *Calvinism in Europe, 1540–1620* (New York: Cambridge University Press, 1997).

Ignatius Loyola and the Jesuits

John O'Malley, *The First Jesuits* (Cambridge: Harvard University Press, 1993).

Thomas Worcester, ed., *The Cambridge Companion to the Jesuits* (Cambridge: Cambridge University Press, 2008).

John Patrick Donnelly, *Ignatius of Loyola: Founder of the Jesuits*, Library of World Biography Series (London: Longman, 2004).

George Schurhammer, *Francis Xavier, His Life, His Times*, 3 vol. (Rome: Jesuit Historical Institute, 1973).

Robert Bireley, *The Jesuits and the Thirty Years War: Kings, Courts, and Confessors* (Cambridge: Cambridge University Press, 2003).

Liam Matthew Brockey, *Journey to the East: The Jesuit Mission to China, 1529–1724* (Cambridge, MA: Belknap Press / Harvard University Press, 2008).

Council of Trent

John O'Malley, *Trent: What Happened at the Council* (Cambridge, MA: Belknap Press/Harvard University Press, 2013).

Robert Bireley, *The Refashioning of Catholicism, 1450–1700: A Reassessment of the Counter Reformation* (Washington, DC: Catholic University of America Press, 1999).

R. Po-Chia Hsia, *World of Catholic Renewal, 1540–1770*, New Approaches to European History 30, 2nd ed. (Cambridge: Cambridge University Press, 2005).

Thomas F. Mayer, *Reforming Reformation, Catholic Christendom, 1300–1700* (Ashgate, 2012).

Anthony D. Wright, *The Counter-Reformation: Catholic Europe and the Non-Christian World*, 2nd ed., series: Catholic Christendom, 1300–1700 (Burlington, VT: Ashgate, 2005).

Gazetteer

Note: Locators show map numbers, not page numbers

Aachen (Aix-la-Chapelle)
Council of Trent 36, 37
Devotio Moderna 3
Great Schism 4
Aarau
Swiss Reformation 26
Aarhus
Reformation in
Scandinavia 29
Abbotsbury
monasteries 30
Aberdeen
English Civil War 58
Scottish Reformation 33
Spanish Armada 47
university 25
Abingdon
monasteries 30
Aden
voyages of discovery 11
Adwalton Moor
English Civil War 57
Agen
Waldensians 2
Agnietenberg
Devotio Moderna 3
Aigues-Vives
Waldensians 2
Aix
archbishopric 10
university 25
Albany
N. American settlers 51
Albergen
Devotio Moderna 3
Albertina
university 25
Albi
French religious wars 44
Waldensians 2
Alcalá
Loyola 39
university 25
Aldbury
monasteries 30
Ales
Waldensians 2
Algie
Europe after 1648 55
Cromwell's foreign wars 59
Algiers
empire of Charles V 14
Jewish persecution 19
All Saints Strait
Magellan's
circumnavigation 13
Allstedt
Melanchthon and reform
20
peasants' war 17
Almelo
Devotio Moderna 3
Alsace
Jewish persecution 19
Amalfi
archbishopric 10
Amazon River
Catholic missions 42

Amersfoort
Devotio Moderna 3
Amersham
Lollards 5
Amiens
Northern Renaissance 9
Amsterdam
Anabaptists 18
Calvinism 27
Christian Europe in 1600
50
Devotio Moderna 3
Dutch Reform 46
Europe after 1648 55
Germany in 1618 52
Jewish persecution 19
Lutheran Germany 22
Melanchthon and reform
20
Netherlands reform 45
Northern Renaissance 9
Peace of Westphalia 54
progress of reform 21
Spanish Armada 47
Thirty Years' War 53
Angers
French religious wars 44
university 25
Angrogna
Reformation in France 28
Anjum
Devotio Moderna 3
Ansbach
Lutheran Germany 22
Antwerp
after the Peace of Augsburg
35
Devotio Moderna 3
Dutch Reform 46
Jewish persecution 19
Lutheran Germany 22
Melanchthon and reform
20
Netherlands reform 45
Northern Renaissance 9
Peace of Westphalia 54
printing 7
Spanish Armada 47
Anzbach
Waldensians 2
Apóstoles
Jesus Reductions 43
Aquileia
archbishopric 10
Arezzo
Italian Renaissance 8
university 1
Arguin
voyages of discovery 11
Arles
Waldensians 2
Arlington
Catholic missions 42
Armagh
archbishopric 10
Arnhem
Devotio Moderna 3
Arnhem-Marienborn
Devotio Moderna 3

Arras
Dutch Reform 46
Arundel
monasteries 30
Aschersleben
Peace of Westphalia 54
Ashbourne
Lollards 5
Ashford
Lollards 5
Aston
Lollards 5
Asunción
Jesus Reductions 43
Auch
archbishopric 10
Waldensians 2
Augsburg
Anabaptists 18
Bucer 24
Council of Trent 36, 37, 38
empire of Charles V 14
Germany in 1618 52
knights' war 16
Luther 15
Melanchthon and reform
20
peasants' war 17
printing 7
progress of reform 21
Austerlitz
Anabaptists 18
Austria
Jewish persecution 19
Avignon
archbishopric 10
Calvinism 27
empire of Charles V 14
French religious wars 44
Great Schism 4
Reformation in France 28
rise of the Jesuits 30
Waldensians 2
Avignonet
Waldensians 2
Azores
voyages of discovery 11
Azuchi
mission to Japan 60

Bagnols
Waldensians 2
Bahia
Catholic missions 42
Bamberg
printing 7
Banbury
Lollards 5
Bangor
Ireland 48
Banská Stiavnica
Hussites 6
Barcelona
after the Peace of Augsburg
35
Christian Europe in 1600
50
empire of Charles V 14
Europe after 1648 55

Jewish persecution 19
Loyola 39
printing 7
Spanish Armada 47
university 1
Bardney
Pilgrimage of Grace 31
Bari
archbishopric 10
Barking
monasteries 30
Barlings
Pilgrimage of Grace 31
Barnard Castle
Pilgrimage of Grace 31
Barnet
Lollards 5
Basel (Basle)
after the Peace of Augsburg
35
Anabaptists 18
Calvin 25
Calvinism 27
Europe after 1648 55
Germany in 1618 52
knights' war 16
Lutheran Germany 22
Melanchthon and reform 20
Northern Renaissance 9
peasants' war 17
printing 7
Swiss Reformation 23, 26
university 1
Bath
Lollards 5
monasteries 30
Baton Rouge
Catholic missions 42
Bavaria
Jewish persecution 19
Bayonne
Jewish persecution 19
Bayreuth
Luther 15
Beaulieu
monasteries 30
Belém
Catholic missions 42
Belfast
Ireland 48
Benevento
archbishopric 10
Benguela
voyages of discovery 11
Bergamo
Waldensians 2
Bergen
Reformation in
Scandinavia 29
Bergum
Devotio Moderna 3
Berlikum
Devotio Moderna 3
Berlin
Council of Trent 36, 37, 38
Europe after 1648 55
Germany in 1618 52
Hussites 6
Lutheran Germany 22

Peace of Westphalia 54
peasants' war 17
progress of reform 21
Reformation in France 28
Bern (Berne)
Calvin 25
Lutheran Germany 22
Melanchthon and reform
20
Swiss Reformation 23, 26
Besançon
archbishopric 10
Northern Renaissance 9
Waldensians 2
Bethlehem (Low Countries)
Devotio Moderna 3
Beverwijk
Devotio Moderna 3
Béziers
Waldensians 2
Biel
Swiss Reformation 23
Birmingham
Lollards 5
Bishop Auckland
Pilgrimage of Grace 31
Blomberg
Devotio Moderna 3
Boblingen
peasants' war 17
Böddeken
Devotio Moderna 3
Bödingen
Devotio Moderna 3
Bodmin
monasteries 30
Bohemia
Jewish persecution 19
Bois-Seigneur-Isaac
Devotio Moderna 3
Bojador, Cape
voyages of discovery 11
Bollène
Waldensians 2
Bologna
Council of Trent 36, 37, 38
printing 7
university 1
Bolton
monasteries 30
Bolzano
peasants' war 17
Bombay (Mumbai)
Francis Xavier 41
Bonn
Devotio Moderna 3
Bordeaux
after the Peace of Augsburg
35
archbishopric 10
Calvinism 27
Cromwell's foreign wars 59
Europe after 1648 55
French religious wars 44
Great Schism 4
Jewish persecution 19
Reformation in France 28
rise of the Jesuits 30
university 1

Bordersholm
Devotio Moderna 3
Bordesley
monasteries 30
Boston (England)
monasteries 30
Puritan migration 49
Boston (Massachusetts)
N. American colonies 56
N. American settlers 51
Bourges
archbishopric 10
French religious wars 44
rise of the Jesuits 30
university 1
Braga
archbishopric 10
Brandenburg
Jewish persecution 19
Bratislava (Pressburg)
Hussites 6
university 1
Braunsberg
rise of the Jesuits 30
Breclav
Anabaptists 18
Breda
Dutch Reform 46
Netherlands reform 45
Bredevoort
Devotio Moderna 3
Breitenfeld
Peace of Westphalia 54
Thirty Years' War 53
Bremen
archbishopric 10
Lutheran Germany 22
Melanchthon and reform
20
Peace of Westphalia 54
progress of reform 21
Brest
Spanish Armada 47
Bridlington
monasteries 30
Pilgrimage of Grace 31
Brielle
Devotio Moderna 3
Brill
Dutch Reform 46
Brindisi
archbishopric 10
Bristol
English Civil War 57, 58
Lollards 5
monasteries 30
Pilgrimage of Grace 31
Puritan migration 49
Spanish Armada 47
voyages of discovery 12
Brixen
peasants' war 17
Brno (Brünn)
Anabaptists 18
Hussites 6
printing 7
Reformation in France 28
rise of the Jesuits 30
Bruges
Dutch Reform 46
Netherlands reform 45
Northern Renaissance 9
printing 7
Spanish Armada 47

Brussels
Calvinism 27
Devotio Moderna 3
Dutch Reform 46
Netherlands reform 45
Northern Renaissance 9
printing 7
Buckland
monasteries 30
Buda
Calvinism 27
Hussites 6
Jewish persecution 19
printing 7
Budapest
empire of Charles V 14
Buenos Aires
Catholic missions 42
voyages of discovery 12
Bungay
monasteries 30
Burford
Lollards 5
Burton on Trent
monasteries 30
Bury St Edmunds
Lollards 5
monasteries 30
Butzbach
Devotio Moderna 3
Byland
monasteries 30

Cadiz
Cromwell's foreign wars 59
Spanish Armada 47
Caen
university 1
Cagliari
archbishopric 10
Italian Renaissance 8
Cahors
university 1
Cairo
voyages of discovery 11
Caister
Pilgrimage of Grace 31
Calais
Dutch Reform 46
Northern Renaissance 9
Cali
Catholic missions 42
Calicut
voyages of discovery 11
Cambrai
Devotio Moderna 3
Dutch Reform 46
Northern Renaissance 9
Cambridge
Bucer 24
Christian Europe in 1600
50
English Reformation 32
Lollards 5
monasteries 30
Northern Renaissance 9
Puritan migration 49
university 1
Camerino
university 1
Canary Islands
Magellan's
circumnavigation 13
voyages of discovery 11

Canterbury
archbishopric 10
English Reformation 32
French religious wars 44
Lollards 5
monasteries 30
Pilgrimage of Grace 31
Canton
Francis Xavier 41
Cape Blanc
voyages of discovery 11
Cape Bojador
voyages of discovery 11
Cape Comorin
Francis Xavier 41
Cape of Good Hope
Magellan's
circumnavigation 13
voyages of discovery 11
Cape Verde Islands
Magellan's
circumnavigation 13
voyages of discovery 11
Capua
archbishopric 10
Caracas
Catholic missions 42
Carlisle
English Reformation 32
Pilgrimage of Grace 31
Carolina
N. American colonies 56
Cartagena
Cromwell's foreign wars 59
Cartmel
Pilgrimage of Grace 31
Cassel
Devotio Moderna 3
Catania
university 1
Cattaro
Jewish persecution 19
Cerea
Waldensians 2
Cerne
monasteries 30
České Budějovice (Budweis)
Hussites 6
Charleston
N. American colonies 56
Chelmo
Devotio Moderna 3
Chelmsford
Lollards 5
Cheriton
English Civil War 58
Chester
English Reformation 32
monasteries 30
Pilgrimage of Grace 31
Chesterton
Lollards 5
Christchurch
monasteries 30
Christiania
Europe after 1648 55
Chur
Swiss Reformation 26
Clermont
Waldensians 2
Coburg
Luther 15
Melanchthon and reform
20

Cockermouth
Pilgrimage of Grace 31
Coggeshall
monasteries 30
Cognac
French religious wars 44
Coimbra
university 1
Colchester
Lollards 5
Pilgrimage of Grace 31
Puritan migration 49
Colmar
Northern Renaissance 9
Cologne (Köln)
archbishopric 10
Bucer 24
Calvinism 27
Christian Europe in 1600
50
Devotio Moderna 3
Dutch Reform 46
empire of Charles V 14
Germany in 1618 52
Jewish persecution 19
knights' war 16
Lutheran Germany 22
Melanchthon and reform 20
peasants' war 17
printing 7
progress of reform 21
university 1
Concepción
Jesus Reductions 43
Concord
N. American settlers 51
Connecticut
N. American colonies 56
Constance (Konstanz)
Swiss Reformation 23, 26
Constantinople (Istanbul)
printing 7
Copenhagen
after the Peace of Augsburg
35
Calvinism 27
Christian Europe in 1600
50
empire of Charles V 14
Europe after 1648 55
printing 7
Reformation in
Scandinavia 29
university 1
Corbarieu
Waldensians 2
Corby
Lollards 5
Córdoba
Catholic missions 42
Corfu
Jewish persecution 19
Cork
Ireland 48
Corpus
Jesus Reductions 43
Corrientes
Jesus Reductions 43
Corunna
Spanish Armada 47
Cosenza
archbishopric 10
Coventry
Lollards 5
monasteries 30

Creake
Lollards 5
Cremona
Jewish persecution 19
Crowland
monasteries 30
Cuzco
Catholic missions 42
voyages of discovery 12

Dalheim
Devotio Moderna 3
Danbury
N. American settlers 51
Danzig (Gdansk)
empire of Charles V 14
Melanchthon and reform
20
Poland 34
printing 7
Darien
Catholic missions 42
Darmstadt
Melanchthon and reform
20
Daventry
Lollards 5
Deerfield
N. American settlers 51
Delaware
N. American colonies 56
Delft
Devotio Moderna 3
Dutch Reform 46
Netherlands reform 45
printing 7
Derby
Lollards 5
Pilgrimage of Grace 31
Puritan migration 49
Derry (Londonderry)
Ireland 48
Dessau
Peace of Westphalia 54
Thirty Years' War 53
Dettingen
Devotio Moderna 3
Deventer
Devotio Moderna 3
Dutch Reform 46
printing 7
Devizes
Lollards 5
Diepenveen
Devotio Moderna 3
Dijon
Calvinism 27
Northern Renaissance 9
Dillingen
rise of the Jesuits 30
Dingle
Ireland 48
Dingwall
Scottish Reformation 33
Doesburg
Devotio Moderna 3
Dôle
rise of the Jesuits 30
university 1
Domazlice
Hussites 6
Dömitz
Peace of Westphalia 54
Doncaster
Pilgrimage of Grace 31

Dongo
Waldensians 2
Dordrecht
Devotio Moderna 3
Dorstadt
Devotio Moderna 3
Dort
Dutch Reform 46
Douai
Dutch Reform 46
university 1
Dover (England)
Lollards 5
Dover (New Hampshire)
N. American settlers 51
Dresden
Europe after 1648 55
Germany in 1618 52
Hussites 6
Luther 15
Lutheran Germany 22
peasants' war 17
Drogheda
Ireland 48
Drosendorf
Waldensians 2
Dublin
after the Peace of Augsburg 35
archbishopric 10
Christian Europe in 1600 50
Cromwell's foreign wars 59
Ireland 48
university 1
Dunkirk
Cromwell's foreign wars 59
Spanish Armada 47
Dunstable (England)
Lollards 5
Dunstable (Massachusetts)
N. American settlers 51
Durham
English Reformation 32
Pilgrimage of Grace 31

Eberhardsklausen
Devotio Moderna 3
Ebernberg
knights' war 16
Edgehill
English Civil War 57
Edinburgh
after the Peace of Augsburg 35
Calvinism 27
Christian Europe in 1600 50
Cromwell's foreign wars 59
empire of Charles V 14
English Civil War 58
printing 7
Scottish Reformation 33
Spanish Armada 47
university 1
Eernstein
Devotio Moderna 3
Eferding
Peace of Westphalia 54
Egmont
Dutch Reform 46
Eindhoven
Devotio Moderna 3
Einsiedeln
Swiss Reformation 23

Eisenach
Melanchthon and reform 20
Eisleben
Luther 15
El Paso
Catholic missions 42
Elblag
Poland 34
Elizabeth
N. American settlers 51
Elizabethsdal
Devotio Moderna 3
Elmina
voyages of discovery 11
Elsegem
Devotio Moderna 3
Elstow
monasteries 30
Embrun
archbishopric 10
Waldensians 2
Emden
Anabaptists 18
Devotio Moderna 3
Dutch Reform 46
Melanchthon and reform 20
Emmerich
Devotio Moderna 3
Erfurt
Luther 15
peasants' war 17
university 1
Esens-Marienkamp
Devotio Moderna 3
Espiritu Santo
Catholic missions 42
Esztergom
archbishopric 10
Hussites 6
Evora
university 1
Ewig
Devotio Moderna 3
Exeter
English Civil War 57, 58
Puritan migration 49
Eye
Lollards 5

Faenza
Waldensians 2
Fairfield
N. American settlers 51
Faringdon
Lollards 5
Farnham
Lollards 5
Faro
printing 7
Ferrara
Italian Renaissance 8
Jewish persecution 19
Loyola 39
university 1
Fez
Jewish persecution 19
Florence (Firenze)
after the Peace of Augsburg 35
empire of Charles V 14
Europe after 1648 55
Italian Renaissance 8
Jewish persecution 19

printing 7
Reformation in France 28
university 1
Waldensians 2
Ford
monasteries 30
Fortaleza
Catholic missions 42
Fountains
monasteries 30
Pilgrimage of Grace 31
Framlingham
Lollards 5
Franeker
university 1
Frankenhausen
peasants' war 17
Frankenthal
Devotio Moderna 3
Frankfurt
Germany in 1618 52
Jewish persecution 19
knights' war 16
Luther 15
Lutheran Germany 22
Peace of Westphalia 54
peasants' war 17
printing 7
university 1
Freiberg
Luther 15
Freiburg
peasants' war 17
university 1
Frenswegen
Devotio Moderna 3
Fribourg
Swiss Reformation 26
Fulda
peasants' war 17
rise of the Jesuits 30
Funay
mission to Japan 60
Furness
monasteries 30

Gaesdonck
Devotio Moderna 3
Gaillac
French religious wars 44
Galway
Ireland 48
Gdansk (Danzig)
Hussites 6
Poland 34
Geneva
after the Peace of Augsburg 35
Anabaptists 18
Calvin 25
Calvinism 27
Christian Europe in 1600 50
Council of Trent 36, 37, 38
Europe after 1648 55
French religious wars 44
Germany in 1618 52
Jewish persecution 19
Lutheran Germany 22
printing 7
Reformation in France 28
Swiss Reformation 23, 25, 26
university 1

Genoa
after the Peace of Augsburg 35
archbishopric 10
Calvinism 27
empire of Charles V 14
Europe after 1648 55
Germany in 1618 52
Italian Renaissance 8
Jewish persecution 19
Reformation in France 28
rise of the Jesuits 30
university 1
Waldensians 2
Ghent
Devotio Moderna 3
Dutch Reform 46
empire of Charles V 14
Netherlands reform 45
Northern Renaissance 9
printing 7
Giessen
Luther 15
Glarus
Swiss Reformation 23, 26
Glasgow
Scottish Reformation 33
university 1
Glastonbury
monasteries 30
Pilgrimage of Grace 31
Glatz
rise of the Jesuits 30
Glogau
Peace of Westphalia 54
Glogow
Poland 34
Gloucester
Lollards 5
monasteries 30
Puritan migration 49
Gniezno (Gnesen)
archbishopric 10
Goa
Francis Xavier 41
voyages of discovery 11
Goldberg
Peace of Westphalia 54
Goslar
Melanchthon and reform 20
Gouda
Devotio Moderna 3
printing 7
Gourdon
Waldensians 2, 26
Grammont
Devotio Moderna 3
Gran
archbishopric 10
Granada
empire of Charles V 14
university 1
Grauhof
Devotio Moderna 3
Gravelines
Spanish Armada 47
Graz
rise of the Jesuits 30
university 1
Greifswald
university 1
Grenoble
French religious wars 44
university 1

Grobbendonk
Devotio Moderna 3
Groenendaal
Devotio Moderna 3
Groningen
Devotio Moderna 3
Dutch Reform 46
Melanchthon and reform 20
Netherlands reform 45
Gruaro
Waldensians 2
Guatemala
Catholic missions 42

Haderslev
Melanchthon and reform 20
Hagenau
Bucer 24
Hailes
monasteries 30
Halberstadt
Devotio Moderna 3
Halesowen
monasteries 30
Halle
Luther 15
Hamar
Reformation in Scandinavia 29
Hamburg
Calvinism 27
Germany in 1618 52
Jewish persecution 19
Loyola 39
Lutheran Germany 22
Melanchthon and reform 20
printing 7
progress of reform 21
Hamersleben
Devotio Moderna 3
Hanover
Europe after 1648 55
Jewish persecution 19
Hardenberg
Devotio Moderna 3
Harderwijk
Devotio Moderna 3
Harlem
Anabaptists 18
Devotio Moderna 3
Dutch Reform 46
printing 7
Hartford
N. American settlers 51
Haskerdijken
Devotio Moderna 3
Haughmond
monasteries 30
Hautpoul
Waldensians 2
Heidelberg
Bucer 24
Christian Europe in 1600 50
Luther 15
Melanchthon and reform 20
progress of reform 21
university 1
Heiningen
Devotio Moderna 3

Index

Note: Locators are page numbers, not map numbers. Numbers in italics indicate illustrations.

Photograph acknowledgments

All photographs © Tim Dowley Associates Ltd except

p. 12:	© Mauro Bighin | Dreamstime.com
p. 13:	© Spaceheater | Dreamstime.com
p. 14:	© Georgios Kollidas | Dreamstime.com
pp. 22/23:	© Neil Harrison | Dreamstime.com
p. 44:	© Stbernardstudio | Dreamstime.com
pp. 50/51:	© Bkaiser | Dreamstime.com
p. 54:	© Ian Danbury | Dreamstime.com
p. 56:	© Hans Klamm | Dreamstime.com
p. 58:	© Weber11 | Dreamstime.com
p. 64:	© Georgios Kollidas | Dreamstime.com
p. 68:	© Andreas Weber | Dreamstime.com
p. 70:	(Zwingli) © Georgios Kollidas | Dreamstime.com
	(Grossmünster) © Tomas1111 | Dreamstime.com
p. 77:	© Hai Huy Ton That | Dreamstime.com
p. 80:	© Ams22 | Dreamstime.com
pp. 94/95:	© Tonino Corso | Dreamstime.com
p. 96:	© Georgios Kollidas | Dreamstime.com
p. 106:	© Pongmanat Tasiri | Dreamstime.com
p. 110:	© Jose Antonio Sánchez Reyes | Dreamstime.com
p. 118:	© Joymsk | Dreamstime.com
pp. 120/121:	© Americanspirit | Dreamstime.com
p. 124:	© Americanspirit | Dreamstime.com
p. 140:	© Amanda Lewis | Dreamstime.com
p. 142:	© Georgios Kollidas | Dreamstime.com
p. 144:	© Tim@awe | Dreamstime.com